Y0-CDI-102

SAVING BASEBALL FROM ITSELF

A Fan's Guide

Howard G. Peretz

© Copyright 2020, Howard G. Perez

All Rights Reserved.

In accordance with the U.S. Copyright Act of 1976, the scanning, up-loading, and electronic sharing of any part of this book without the permission of the publisher constitute unlawful privacy and theft of the author's intellectual property. If you would like to use material from the book (other than for preview purposes), prior written permission must be obtained by contacting the publisher at the address below. Thank you for your support of the author's rights.

ISBN: 978-1-94863-805-0

Cotact the author at: PeretzHoward@gmail.com

Or visit the author's websites for more information:

www.SavingBaseball.net

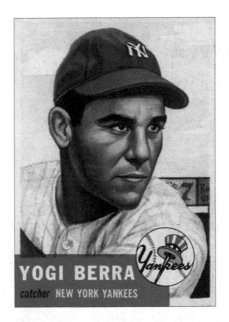

YOGI BERRA
catcher NEW YORK YANKEES

*"If people don't want to come to the ballpark,
how are you going to
stop them."*

—Yogi Berra

*Yogi, of course, never envisioned COVID-19 would force the 2020 season
if — the longest word in the English language — played will be crowd-less.*

*"It's unbelievable how much you don't know
about the game you've been playing your whole life."*
— Mickey Mantle

*"Every day is a new opportunity.
You can build on yesterday's success
or put its failures behind and start over again.
That's the way life is, with a new game every day,
and that's the way baseball is."*
— Bullet Bob Feller

*"Well it took me 17 years to get 3,000 hits in baseball,
and I did it one afternoon on the golf course."*
— Hank Aaron

TABLE OF CONTENTS

ACKNOWLEGEMENTS

To my late Dad Milton J. Peretz, who returned home from serving in the Navy on the Doyle C. Barnes in WWII and took me to Yankee Stadium when I was eight years of age; started my love affair with baseball.

Many thanks to Don Drooker who supplied many of the images you'll see in the book. Don is a sports memorabilia expert and a top-rated eBay seller who can be found on that platform under ID: rotisserieduck. Don also shares his thoughts on the game on his blog at rotisserieduckduck.com

Robin Surface at Fideli Publishing, hardly a sports fan but a passionate and knowledgeable expert on all things self-publishing. Happily she spends my money as if it was hers, proving Midwestern values reside in Indiana are for real.

Stephanie Straub of the HF Group also a Hoosier, knows all of the ins and outs of digital printing. She treats me like a big customer, meeting all delivery requirements without sacrificing quality. Importantly, didn't laugh at me when I suggested a flip book.

Writing a book during COVID-19 while waiting to see whether the 2020 baseball season would be played turned out to be particularly challenging. I thank the discipline of **persistence** for getting me through.

JOHN WOODEN

I remember hearing John Wooden, The Wizard of Basketball say, "Of all the sports, basketball has by far the biggest ball, lending itself to television viewing." This was back in the 1970s when the NBA was still in its infancy, and Wooden was sure basketball would become the number-one sports in the USA.

That may still happen, after all the guy was a visionary and a legend. While he was at UCLA he won 620 games in 27 seasons and 10 NCAA titles during his last 12 seasons, including seven in a row from 1967 to 1973. His UCLA teams also established a NCAA men's basketball record winning streak of 88 games and four perfect 30–0 seasons.

INTRODUCTION

I have written several well received all-sports history books dating to 1999 and was planning to publish a new text focusing solely on baseball. I have given myself the title of Old School Sports Junkie as I am both old in the tooth (80 years young) and a believer in corny sports traditions-"take me out to the ballgame" for example is my ringtone. While researching the subject and writing the preface pre-COVID-19 it became apparent that baseball was floundering losing the game both on and off the field. My response was to change directions, and utilize my meager skill set for a more noble pursuit: *Saving Baseball from Itself.* This white paper is my version of a "Tell-All Book" but unlike Jim Bouton's *Ball Four,* I first take the game apart for failure to read the strike zone, then I put "Humpty Dumpty" together again.

The NFL is now the most popular sport in the country, baseball a distant second, and in the rear-view mirror third place NBA closing. MLB seems confused as to what to do to take back that number-one spot, apart from playing the 2020 condensed season at all costs. The sign stealing scandal has hurt the sport but is just a short-term distraction that will go away by the 2021 season. The issue with MLB management is either: their inability to recognize the seriousness of the problem, hiding behind yearly revenue growth and franchise value appreciation, or a deep down feeling the game is no longer viable for today's 21th Century 24/7 consumer.

My question is two part: Does MLB in its gut believe in the future of baseball, and do the empty suits at MLB headquarters on Park Avenue really love the game?

I wish I knew the answer to this question. Instead, MLB deals with the margins and plays defense. There should be no sacred cows, including baseball as our "National Pastime."

CHAPTER ONE

HOOKED ON BASEBALL SINCE THE VERY BEGINNING

I have loved baseball since my dad took me to Yankee Stadium to see the home team in 1947 when I was eight years old. About that same time, I was enchanted by "Casey at the Bat: A Ballad of the Republic Sung in the Year 1888." I was heartsick when I came to the same ending after each read; I always hoped that Casey would be the hero. "But there is no joy in Mudville — mighty Casey has struck out."

According to my parents, my first spoken word was ball, not Mom. My memories of baseball are as vivid today as they were when I was making them. Each year of my boyhood, adolescence, and even early adulthood, is filled with visits to the stadium. I have lots of fond memories, including touching the monuments at Memorial Park in center field. I loved seeing the list of names: Manager Miller Huggins, Babe Ruth, Lou Gehrig and Joe DiMaggio, Owner George Steinbrenner and Mantle added later; Jeter will be next.

George Will, known as a high-brow political commentator and baseball lover, said it most eloquently: "Baseball, it is said, is only a game. True. And the Grand Canyon is only a hole in Arizona (my home state).

Not all holes, or games, are created equal." I had so many cherished moments at Yankee Stadium, "The Cathedral of Baseball

- Waiting for the bell then leading the Yankees out of their first base dugout with the game about to start

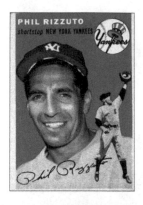

I remember seeing "Scooter" Rizzuto (I liked the name Scooter so much that I gave it to my beloved dachshund).

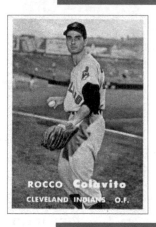

I remember being chased by Rocky Colavito, the Indians All-Star right fielder, after taunting him throughout a Sunday daytime doubleheader for always flexing his muscles and taking too long to release his powerful throwing arm.

- Forcing postage paid self-addressed postcards through players' car windows in the hopes of getting them autographed. (They parked alongside the ballpark on the first base side.)

- Losing a souvenir to an elderly woman who caught the ball in her lap with the skirt of her dress.

- Eating cold leftover hamburger sandwiches made and packed by my Yiddish grandmother after taking a bus and subway. (I was just 12 years old when I started this practice of leaving at 10 a.m. and returning around 9 p.m. without any worries about something bad happening to me on these solo outings.)

- Watching reliever Ryne Duren, who wore "Coke bottle" glasses, throw warm-up pitches to the backstop and flatten 6'4" 240-lb. Indians first sacker Luke Easter, who was frozen at the plate.

- Catching a bag of peanuts thrown accurately from a far-away "celebrity" vendor.
- Sneaking in and not paying for a reserved seat ticket because Patty, one of my Dad's wartime pals, was a ticket taker. (We shook his hand and he pretended to take our ticket.)
- Religiously filling out a scorecard with a shortened pencil with no eraser.

I remember walking lefty "Steady" Eddie Lopat up the hill to the splendid Grand Concourse (Blvd.) to the Concourse Plaza Hotel, his home away from home, along with Charlie "King Kong" Keller among others.

CASEY STENGEL

I remember when the Yankees were so good, some would say arrogant, that when Manager Casey Stengel sent Joe Collins up to bat to sacrifice bunt the runner to second, Collins missed the sign and instead hit a 2-run walk-off homer for the win. The following day "The Old Professor" Stengel fined him for missing that sign. Stengel in addition to winning four World Series Championships to go along with 10 AL pennants was known for speaking "Stengelese." For example, he'd say, "All line up alphabetically according to size."

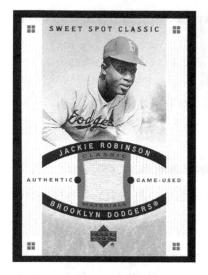

I remember seeing Yogi Berra tag out Jackie Robinson during game one of the 1955 World Series. (I had a great view behind the 3rd base dugout when he attempted to steal home only to be called safe — Berra had the plate blocked — but more importantly, the Yankees behind Whitey "The Chairman of the Board" Ford won.)

I remember attending Old Timer's Day, started by a two-inning exhibition between retired players before the real game started.

That game, I got to watch one of my dad's heroes — Joe DiMaggio, "The Yankee Clipper."

DiMaggio was always introduced as "baseball's greatest living player" by public address announcer Bob Sheppard, who held that post for 56 seasons.

- I remember Frank "The Crow" Crosetti touching the 3rd base bag at the end of every home inning. He was 3rd base Coach for 20-consecutive seasons after 17 as the shortstop.

- And, waiting for reliever Joe Page to hop over the right field fence after leaving the pen and walk deliberately to the mound with his jacket over his shoulder, until the bat boy came out to take it.

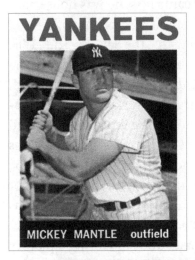

My favorite memory of all is cheering Mickey Mantle batting left-handed, bad legs and all, hitting a walk-off home run in game three of the 1964 World Series on a flattened knuckle ball first pitch from Cards' Barney Schultz.

I often would get into small weekly skirmishes with schoolmates and neighbors about who was the better position player among the 3 NYC teams — the Yankees, the Dodgers, and the Giants. I usually chose Mays, Snider or Mantle (Willie, Mickey and the Duke) as well as Campanella or Berra, Hodges vs. Skowron, Dark vs. Pee Wee Reese or Rizzuto. The only drawback of rooting for the Pinstripes was we won almost all of the time, not preparing me for life's marathon roller coaster ride that included losses.

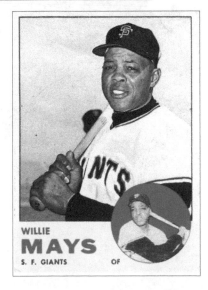

The Polo Grounds, a short walk across the bridge from Yankee Stadium in Manhattan where the Giants played also has special meaning. I hated the Brooklyn Dodgers, so I rooted for their NL rival the New York Giants. I remember rushing home from middle school to catch Bobby Thomson's 1951 walk-off home run, dubbed "The Little Miracle of Coogan's Bluff." It was the greatest finish in baseball history. Seconds before my schoolmate Howard Schwartz, a Dodgers fan and traitor residing in "Da Bronx," called to exclaim his beloved bums were about to win the pennant. Schwartz was so upset about his team's loss, he was not seen in class for several days and wouldn't accept homework assignments.

Another highlight was playing stick ball with "The Say Hey Kid" Willie Mays on Sugar Hill, the historic district behind the ballpark in Harlem. Stick ball was our favorite pastime. Hitting a pink Spalding punch ball over handball courts in the North quadrant in Parkchester, the community where we lived, was great fun. If you cleared four walls, you had hit a home run. Leroy, our building porter at 89 Metropolitan Oval, was

kind enough to rescue would-be bats on their way to the garbage for my arsenal. These included brooms and carpet sweepers for my arsenal. I also must admit to tearing-up every year as I watched Gary Cooper play "Ironman" Lou Gehrig in the 1942 MGM movie Pride of the Yankees. The tears really flowed when Gehrig delivered his July 4, 1939 Farewell Address; "...yet today, I consider myself the luckiest man on the face of the earth."

CHAPTER TWO

BASEBALL IS NO LONGER THE ONLY GAME IN TOWN

Professional baseball started way back in 1886, and dominated through the 1920s because there was no other team sport competition, apart from college football which traces its origins to the 1869 Princeton vs. Rutgers game. (Knute Rockne's 1924 Notre Dame team featuring "The Four Horseman of the Apocalypse" was a seminal moment historically popularized by Grantland Rice, the best sportswriter of his generation. Opening day of the college season didn't begin until the leaves began falling.)

Bart Giamatti, 7th MLB Commissioner in 1989 and a passionate advocate of the game, had this to say: "It breaks your heart. The game begins in the spring when everything else begins again, and it blossoms in the summer, filling the afternoons and evenings, and then as soon as the chill rains come, it stops and leaves you to face the fall alone."

The spring and summer are no longer the exclusive property of MLB. Pre-COVID-19, the 2020 baseball season was scheduled to open March 26, with college basketball's "March Madness" to run from March 17 to April 7. The NBA playoffs the 'real' season, when defense is actually played, was scheduled to run April 18 to June 21. Competition for hockey's Stanley Cup with the lure of sudden-death overtime dramas normally begins in early April. Soccer's MLS league is scheduled from February through October. Even the XFL, the football league from WWE, was planning to relaunch spring football starting in February.

Additionally, there are a slew of classic top-tier individual events typically competing for attention in the Spring and Summer: the Kentucky Derby (part of Racing's Triple Crown, along with the Preakness and the Belmont Stakes), the Indy 500, Nathan's Hot Dog Eating Contest, The Masters, Wimbledon, and the United States Tennis Open. The NFL, literally the elephant in the room, has always started preseason games in late July, highlighted by the Hall of Fame game in Canton, Ohio on or about August 6, with opening day of the regular season is on the first Thursday in September.

When entering childhood as a fan in the Big Apple we had all of the sports in our 'hood. There were far fewer teams in the leagues but the seasons magically flowed seamlessly from one sport to another; baseball spring/summer, football in the fall, and basketball and hockey in the winter.

Apart from baseball, the other professional leagues in post-WWII America struggled to gain traction. College basketball was huge at Madison Square Garden, with doubleheaders and sometimes triple headers, which ended in 1951 as a result of defending National Champion CCNY the neighborhood school succumbing to the point shaving scandal.

The Knicks were relegated to the 69th Street Regiment Armory, a small venue with an even smaller two-digit scoreboard. (One hundred points by a team was rare in those days, but if that lofty number was reached, the scoreboard read 00.)

The league was so weak that stars like the Celtics' Bill Russell doubled as Player/Coaches to save salaries. NBA doubleheaders were standard fare with teams rotating staying in the same location.

The Rangers hockey team was always in the cellar, one of the original six (1942). Since they played on Wednesday and Sunday evenings, school nights, we went instead to see the minor league New York Rovers playing Saturday matinees at Madison Square Garden (MSG).

To watch a top-rated college football game, we had to journey north to see Army at West Point, New York. Army was a national powerhouse and it was thrilling to see Bill "The Lonesome End" Carpenter line up well outside of the huddle, a radical concept not previously seen. Football's Giants, had to play in Yankee Stadium, which was configured for baseball and smallish crowds. All of that changed on December 28, 1958 during the NFL Championship Game when they lost to the Baltimore Colts in overtime. It became known as "The Greatest Game Ever Played."

I sat in the wooden center field bleachers setting them on fire with other fans to keep warm as Johnny Unitas

BILL CARPENTER

tas marched his team down field toward my end of the stadium — the open end. Johnny's magic, referred to as the first two-minute scoring drive, tied the contest with 7 seconds remaining in regulation play on Steve Myra's 20-yard field goal.

All in attendance,

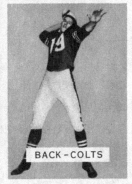

John Unitas   BACK - COLTS

including the participants, thought the game ended in a tie, but the league decided to play its first overtime, which the Colts won. To this day I am convinced the Giants' running back, Frank Gifford, had a first down which would have decided the game, but the referees were more concerned with attending to the Colts All-Star defensive end, Gino Marchetti, who broke his leg on the play. I can still see him lying on the stretcher under the other goal post because he didn't want to miss the action.

This was the first NFL game to be televised nationally. It's unbelievable to realize that the NFL's rise to popularity began in a baseball stadium — "The House That Ruth Built."

CHAPTER THREE

THE NFL HAS BECOME OUR NEW "NATIONAL PASTIME"

The NFL, partially as a result of gambling, has moved well ahead of MLB in popularity — polling 34% to 16%. Fantasy football participation is a whopping 78% vs. 39% for baseball. Moreover, Nevada sportsbooks show revenues from football at $384.6 million, with baseball coming in at $22.5.

At the conclusion of the NFL's 100th regular season in 2019, the San Francisco 49ers defeated the Seattle Seahawks by mere inches as time expired. The voice of sports, Al Michaels, put the nail in the MLB coffin, by saying to his play-by-play sidekick Chris Collinsworth, "The NFL has become the national pastime."

LAMAR HUNT

Commissioner Pete Rozelle (1960–1989) was a Los Angeles publicity whiz rather than another attorney. He pushed the league to dominance beginning with the first Super Bowl in 1967. Of interest was the term Super Bowl, conceived by the Kansas Chiefs owner and founder Lamar Hunt after watching his children play with a "super ball."

Key elements of the league's success included:

- MNF (1970) the brainchild of ABC's Roone Arledge, demonstrating football could exist beyond Sunday afternoon by pairing "Humble" Howard Cosell, Frank Gifford and "Dandy" Don Meredith in the booth.

- Revenue sharing among all clubs, mostly from television, when combined with a hard salary cap in 1994, allowed small market teams like the Green Bay Packers and Buffalo Bills to compete with the big boys.

- Fast-talking Mel Kiper Jr., took the draft from a 1936 obscure non-media story to a three-day prime time television bonanza.

- The draft (April 23-25) is evidence of the NFL's skill in keeping the sport front and center between seasons — it occurs during the heart of the normal baseball season. (Funny, I was in the military during the Vietnam War

MEL KIPLER JR.

  and the word draft (card) still sends chills down by spine.)

- Free agency signings in March, scouting combine in late February —affectionately referred to as the "Underwear Olympics," OTA's and mini-camps in the Spring, HOF ceremonies and the beginning of preseason games in August, regular season start September 10.

- The CBA agreement with players is approved to 2030. The new CBA also adds an additional 17th game to the schedule and increases playoff teams from 12 to 14.

Although there have been many bumps in the road under the stewardship of Commissioner Roger Goodell, the league has effectively navigated through a range of low to mid-level hurdles:

- dealing with injuries from concussions by implementing mandatory sideline concussion exams managed by an independent medical staff,

- settling lawsuits by former players,

- researching the subject of what causes concussions while working on helmet safety,

- after a rough start, tackling domestic violence through painful standardized punishments,

- penalizing the New England Patriots and the greatest QB of all-time Tom Brady in the "Deflategate" scandal,

- reaching a new understanding with the NFLPA after excessive police force by white officers led to the murder of George Floyd an African-American in Minneapolis,

- accepting players kneeling during the National Anthem, a practice started by Colin Kaepernick,

- and changing rules to promote scoring while simultaneously appealing to player safety, protecting the quarterback at all costs.

GEORGE ORWELL

The American sports fan loves to watch violence in action, especially when it includes large bodied, highly skilled, and physically fit specimens The NFL delivers this big time. Baseball by contrast is a non-contact sport. As the late English novelist George Orwell, author of Animal Farm and 1984, said in his December 1945 London Tribune article "The Sporting Spirit," "....sports is war without the tanks."

CHAPTER FOUR

BASEBALL POPULARITY TRENDING DOWNWARD WITH NO REAL FIX IN SIGHT

According to *Forbes Magazine,* baseball revenues have increased for 15 consecutive years, surpassing ten billion for the first time in 2017. COVID-19 in 2020 will obviously erase this trend but the league, based upon its prior behavior, will continue as is. The virus, after all, is an external factor and a once in a lifetime occurrence.

Yet, below the top-line numbers, baseball has serious long-term shortcomings. First, of all the major team sports, baseball's television average audience age is the oldest at 57 years, followed by college football and basketball at 52, the NFL at 50; the NHL at 49; and the NBA at 42. Ballpark attendance has likewise demonstrated declining numbers. For the first time since 2003 total attendance in 2018 fell below 70 million; 69.625 million to be exact for an average of 28,830 per game down 4% from the previous year when the game average was 30,642. Baseball blames unusually bad weather in April for these numbers, but ignores additional postseason games.

A further knock to baseball is the game lacks national superstars. An ESPN study in 1999 naming the greatest athletes of the 20th Century with an emphasis on North American athletes had 19 baseball players ranked in the top 100:

#2-Babe Ruth

#8-Willie Mays

#14 Hank Aaron

#15-Jackie Robinson

#16-Ted Williams

#20-Ty Cobb

#22-Joe DiMaggio

#34-Lou Gehrig

#37-Mickey Mantle

#42-Sandy Koufax

#56-Pete Rose

#60-Walter Johnson

#61-Stan Musial

#62-Bob Gibson

#71-Roberto Clemente

#73-Josh Gibson

#77-Cy Young

#83-Honus Wagner

#89-Rogers Hornsby

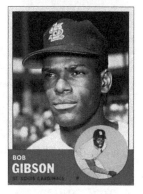

Note: Michael Jordan finished at number one.

By comparison, 2019 ESPN did a related study of the most popular athletes in the world, and apart from soccer, United States athletes were well represented. The study rated popularity on the basis of three variables: endorsements, search score really Google mention and social media followers. Here, of the top 20, shockingly but not surprising, not a single baseball player was mentioned. "King" LeBron James was second following European soccer star Christiano Ronaldo; joining James were: Kevin Durant, Tiger Woods, and Stephen Curry.

Baseball whether by accident or purpose has promoted team visibility over individual stars, which in a perfect world is how I would vote as a fan; of course, my Yankees don't have player names on the back of their jerseys.

CHAPTER FIVE

BASEBALL IS PREVENTED FROM GETTING ITS ACT TOGETHER

T he COVID-19 Virus understandably consumed all of the leagues attention, billions would be lost without a season, as MLB fought tooth and nail with the Major League Baseball Players Association (MLBPA) to get a product on the field. Negotiations painfully displayed publicly through the media by the two sides MLB and MLBPA, not partners but sides, started on March 12, 2020 and didn't end until June 15. As Sports Illustrated commented on the labor unrest evidenced by both parties; "Everyone loses." The result a shortened 60-game season over 65-days followed by the postseason, opening day July 24 the shortest season since 1878. COVID-19 still looms, there is hot spot spiking and a second wave in early fall is probable according to Dr. Anthony Fauci Director of the NIAID. Interestingly, Fauci threw out the first pitch, although on a bounce, on Opening Day at Nationals Park. He was the Captain of the 1958 NYC Regis High School basketball team. Apart from 'play ball' in 2020, baseball has other short-term problems that will need attention.

SIGN STEALING SCANDAL

On January 19, 2020 MLB issued its report on sign stealing involving the Houston Astros in 2017 and 2018. The league took serious action, handing out one-year suspensions for Astros field Manager AJ Hinch and GM Jeff Luhnow, coupled with a $5 million team fine — the largest permissible — and the loss of first and second round draft picks in 2020

MANAGER **ALEX CORA**

and 2021. Red Sox Manager Alex Cora, former bench coach for the Astros, was dismissed shortly thereafter.

While baseball acted decisively, many open wounds remain. Individual Astros players were not punished, with MLB citing their need to grant the players immunity to break the case open, plus predictable resistance by the Major League Baseball Players Association (MLBPA).

How the Astros would be received when they took the field this upcoming season was of major concern. With no fans in the ballpark in 2020, though, the Astros will get a pass. However, sign stealing in theory still has to be eliminated once and for all.

Al Worthington
NEW YORK GIANTS, PITCHER

An opinion piece in *Sports Illustrated* commented that while technology changed how cheating could be accomplished, the drive to gain an edge is engraved in the sport. Cheating dates to 1899, when binoculars were used by the Phillies to steal signs. In 1959, Giants pitcher Al Worthington, a deeply religious man, went to Manager Bill Rigney and asked to be traded because he'd observed teammates cheating. Rigney obliged, and Worthington went to the Chicago White Sox, where he discovered widespread cheating as well.

EDDIE GAEDEL

"Sport Shirt" Bill Veeck, baseball's greatest promoter, owned the Cleveland Indians, St. Louis Browns and White Sox's teams. He bragged in *The Hustler's Handbook* that he took advantage of every opportunity to win. Veeck, who is best remembered for sending 3'7" midget Eddie Gaedel to bat in 1961, also admitted to moving the outfield fence, which was built on rollers, by as much as 15' depending upon the slugging power of the opposition.

PETE ROSE HALL OF FAME BAN

Rose the games' leading career hitter in hits, and nicknamed "Charlie Hustle" because he went all out on every play. Rose admitted in his 2004 autobiography, *My Prison Without Bars*, to betting with illegal bookmakers, and said, "I always bet on the Reds to win."

Baseball's original sin is the Black Sox scandal. Eight players were banned from the game, including All-Star "Shoeless" Joe Jackson, for throwing the 1919 World Series.

Given its gambling history, baseballs penalties are severe. Rose received a lifetime ban from entrance to the Hall of Fame. He refiled for reinstatement recently, citing other violations such as use of steroids and sign stealing as much worse than his transgression.

Ironically, baseball is now in on the gambling business as a result of the 2018 Supreme Court ruling that struck down the law that banned commercial sports betting. The league, not concerned about the perception of hypocrisy, inked an $80 million deal with MGM Resorts International making them their Official Gaming Partner.

Rob Manfred, baseball's 10th Commissioner, said, "Our research is really strong on the idea that sports gaming can be an important source of fan engagement."

IS THE BASEBALL JUICED?

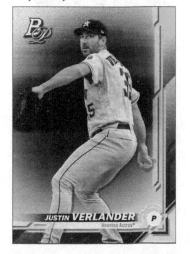

MLB answers no to this question. Astros pitcher Justin Verlander, Future Hall of Fame pitcher and 2-time Cy Young Award winner, claims differently. Why else would baseball have purchased Rawlings in 2018 from Newell Brands, the exclusive supplier of baseballs? Verlander further argues the league has been using juiced baseballs in the Home Run Derby for years.

On the other hand, Five Thirty Eight's research analysis suggests that while home runs are significantly up, the ratio of strikeouts has remained constant — 6.1 strikeouts per homer in 2019 vs. 6.1 in 1920, the beginning of the live ball age.

Babe Ruth, who is given credit for ending the Dead Ball Era, said, "If I'd tried for them dinky singles, I would have batted around six hundred."

Historians trace the live ball era to six factors; changes in ball construction, outlawing certain pitches (chiefly the spitball), more baseballs being used per game, keeping of stats and rule changing, shortening the outfield dimensions, and Babe Ruth's free-swinging hitting style.

WILL MINOR LEAGUE BASEBALL SURVIVE?

Responding to baseball's plan to eliminate minor league clubs including the Appalachian League, several members of Congress started a task force to "save minor league baseball." In total, there are 261 teams bringing the game to small town America, an important core fan base for baseball.

Money is the issue. MLB subsidizes the minor league games, and seasonal player salaries can be as little as $1,100 monthly. COVID-19 has accelerated the demise, and when minor league baseball returns in 2021 it will look entirely different.

CAN THE TAMPA BAY RAYS STAY IN TAMPA BAY?

The expansion Tampa Bay Rays founded in 1998 with an abundance of good young talent and playing competitively in the AL East never drew flies at their home field. The Tampa Bay Rays have been seeking to play half of their home games in Montreal, Canada, since the city once had a professional team, the Montreal Expos (1969–2004).

Tampa Bay has been pushing for a new stadium, Ybor to replace the flawed "The Trop" — the only indoor stadium without a retractable roof in the game. It's hard to imagine a need for an indoor field, but Floridians know it rains in Florida almost every day in the summer.

There will be no new park, and the Rays will honor their lease commitment that runs through 2027. At the moment, the sharing plan between Tampa Bay and Montreal is planned to start in the 2028 season.

PROTECTIVE NETTING

After spectators were injured by foul balls, baseball had no choice but to embark on a campaign to have all 30 teams extend protective netting well beyond home plate to cover all of the entire round. Former commissioner Bud Selig and current commissioner Manfred have been deposed to testify in a three-year-old Wrigley Field injury case.

While safety is paramount, it is but another reason to watch the game from the comforts of your "Man Cave." Of all the major sports, only hockey has fan protective glass, with panels 75" tall covering patrons in the first few rows.

LENGTH OF GAME

Haters of baseball say watching the game is like "watching grass grow." The league has apparently agreed with those critics, forming a committee originally headed by special assistant to the commissioner Joe Torre, ex-Yankees Manager and former All-Star third baseman.

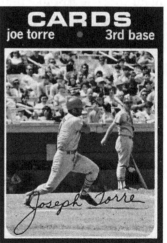

The committee has effectively instituted new rules to speed up the pace of the game. The average game now approaches three hours, which appears to be the tipping point.

The question to be answered is: Will a game shortened by 15 minutes make any difference?

CHAPTER SIX

MAJOR LEAGUE BASEBALL AT THE CROSSROADS

"Some say our national pastime is baseball. Not me. It's gossip."
— Erma Bombeck, American humorist.

O ne of my favorite signature lines when I talk to young audiences that have no sense of time and aging is: "I'm so old I remember when T-shirts only came in all-white." Not to be an alarmist, but baseball could go the way of white T-shirt, unless it takes immediate pro-active measures.

As a well-known German proverb states: "Nothing in this world is permanent." Baseball will never disappear but it could be headed for downsizing. Things like newer new ballparks put on hold, elimination of unprofitable teams — mostly from small markets, shorter seasons, lower ticket prices (a good thing), smaller rosters, the disappearance of minor league baseball, and fewer scouts, coaches, instructors and office staff. All of these, coupled with the decline in franchise values and lower player salaries all point to downsizing being necessary.

In my opinion, downsizing to avoiding disappearance is an art form that is rarely successful. Once the dominoes start falling, they rarely stop. Examples to back this supposition include:

- White Castle founded in 1927 the first fast-food chain now with only 377 locations vs. McDonald's worldwide at 37 855;

- FW Woolworth, the original five and dime store started in Utica, New York in 1879, had 5,000 stores at its peak and ended operations in 2009;

- Sperry Rand's Univac division was first in computers; their commercial mainframe computers debuted in 1951, then along came IBM's 360 family in the early 1960s and Univac's ballgame was over.

- Category killer superstores like Toys R Us have been replaced by Walmart, Amazon and other internet sellers that now capture 11.9% of total sales;

- Shopping malls are on life support, and Mom and Pop retailers becoming endangered species.

While being the first major American sport counts for something, baseball will have to change to survive. There are also many examples of sports ventures that have vanished from the American scene.

- Miniature golf in the 1930s had over 25,000 locations; today a fraction remains.

- In 1934, Lou Gehrig was the first athlete to appear on a cereal box— Wheaties, the Breakfast of Champions. Wheaties is now only a minor brand, with Honey Nut Cheerios taking the number-one spot in ready-to-eat cereals.

- The World's Greatest Athlete competition — the Olympics' Decathlon — won by America's Jim Thorpe and Bruce Jenner, is now an obscure Summer Olympics venue. This is probably due to the competition encompassing ten events spread over two days — it's not designed for today's need for rapid response platforms. We're all about the 100-yard sprint now.

- Indoor Six-Day Cycling at Madison Square Garden circa 1891. My Dad went regularly and the fan base was as enthusiastic as hockey.

- Weekly televised club prize fights on Wednesday and Friday nights have given way to infrequent HBO, Showtime and pay-per-view Saturday night showings. It was not uncommon for fighters to lace them up only every 4-6 weeks.

- The NIT, formerly the major college basketball tournament in the land, was replaced by "March Madness," building a second-tier tournament of teh NCAA leftovers.

- *Sports Illustrated* magazine has been sold once again, this time to Authentic Brands Group. They are intent on building the SI brand, not magazine circulation.

- Professional soccer is still significantly more popular outside the United States. (I saw Brazilian soccer star Pele play for the New York Cosmos of the defunct North American Soccer League on June 15, 1975 at the New Jersey Meadowlands.)

- Bowl Championship Series (BCS), designed to award a national college football championship, is destroying other lesser bowl games. As it stands now, there are 40 corporate-named bowls.

- Volleyball and roller derby never gained traction.

- Women's sports are more popular than ever, but still require subsidization.

- The student athlete is no longer a treasured concept — athlete compensation has become too compelling to be ignored.

REVENUE GROWTH CAN MASK THE EXTENT OF THE PROBLEM

I had a relevant high-profile consulting assignment in the 1980s with "The Greatest Show on Earth." The origin of the circus dates back to April 10, 1871. As with MLB, Ringling Bros. Barnum and Bailey revenues went up each and every year, but this was due to increases in per capita concession revenue from programs, lights, snow cones and cotton candy. The revenue growth was hiding the long-term trend of declining attendance.

My recommendation was the "Americanization of the Circus." I wanted to replace unknown, superb Eastern European circus generational family performers like trapeze artists, with fresh, slightly less skilled American talent. As the greatest public relations hustler of all-time, P.T. Barnum would have said: Americans cheering for Americans is extremely more popular, and hence more salable. It would have resulted in "putting asses in the seats."

Kenneth Feld, son of the modern-day circus savior Irving Feld, rejected this recommendation as not in the tradition of a three-ring circus. On May 21, 2017, the circus literally folded its tent. This was not due to cruelty to animals or competition from the likes of Cirque du Soleil. It was because of lack of interest and consumers moving on to something else.

An annual family visit to the "Big Top" became once every three years, and then it was forgotten. People who worked at the circus loved it much like we love baseball and would often say, "May every day be a circus day."

CHAPTER SEVEN

CHANGING THE ROLE OF THE BASEBALL COMMISSIONER

MLB® COMMISSIONER
ROB MANFRED

R ob Manfred, the very capable and congenial Commissioner of MLB, is not having a good season. Before COVID-19 forced him to publicly fight with the MLBPA over the 2020 condensed season, he was heavily criticized for the handling of the Astros sign stealing season — penalties didn't go far enough — and for referring to the World Series trophy as a "piece of metal." He is currently operating under a contract extension through 2024. He is highly praised by the owners he works for, and with the Collective Bargaining Agreement (CBA) up for renewal in 2021, which is his area of expertise, he would appear to be safe at the plate without needing to slide.

I must admit to not being a big fan of lawyers running the show, including: Manfred at MLB, Adam Silver at the NBA, and Gary Bettman at the NHL. In my experience, which is somewhat dated, an attorney's focus is not on advising you on what you can do, but rather on what you cannot do. They are risk averse, and lacking in creative flair. They'll charge you for phone conversations over 10 minutes in duration, plus travel time.

Before my daughter became a successful practicing attorney, I used to have a stable of lawyer jokes. But, once she passed the bar, I promised her I would refrain. The only quick joke I sneak in now and then is: "What is the difference between a good lawyer and a great one?" Answer: A good lawyer knows the law, the great one knows the judge!" It's amazing that who you know over what you know still counts in every endeavor.

The first baseball commissioner was a former federal judge named Kenesaw Mountain Landis, 1920–1944, who came into power following the 1919 World Series. Known as the "Black Sox Scandal," eight members of the Chicago White Sox received lifetime bans for fixing games. Baseball, therefore, needed a "sheriff in town" to purge gambling interests, and made a smart choice in selecting a high-profile former judge. Said Landis: "Baseball is something more than a game to an American boy. It is his training field for life's work. Destroy his faith in its squareness and honesty and you have planted suspicion of all things in his heart."

JUDGE LANDIS

Baseball today needs a seller/marketer who can "work across the aisle" with the players as well as be a fan first (this is of paramount importance). Someone similar to the 7th commissioner of the game, Bartlett Giamatti. He was a passionate Red Sox fan who served only 1 year in the position. At just 51 years of age, he suffered a heart attack while in office.

With current commissioner Manfred seemingly in trouble, the boo-birds are out and the sports media has predictably devel-

A. BARTLETT GIAMATTI

oped a list of well-known baseball personalities to replace him, including Joe Torre, Bob Costas, David Cone, Bobby Valentine and Doug

MARK CUBAN

Glanville. My initial choice is Mark Cuban because he checks all of the boxes: owner of the NBA Dallas Mavericks; "Shark Tank" ABC television series original investor and co-host; entrepreneur extraordinaire — #179 on Fortune's top 500 list; self-made success story and a dynamic personality. Most significantly he is a fan first owner. He sits at Maverick games in a court-side seat, not in a corporate suite, wearing jeans and a T-shirt and rooting as hard as he can for his team. Regarding this behavior, he says, "I've been a 'Mavs fan for my entire life…I just didn't think that because I bought the team I would change who I am or change how I act."

Cuban has also tried, without success, to purchase three Major League baseball franchises — Cubs, Dodgers, and Mets. The outspoken Cuban also appears to have his eye on the White House. I would vote for him, but 2024 is the earliest this could happen, and baseball needs an immediate blast of fresh air.

TONY CLARK

In thinking further, while Cuban would be a wonderful replacement, the real problem is with the role of the commissioner itself. Currently the commissioner works exclusively for the owners *not* the game. Because of this, it's no wonder MLBPA Executive Director Tony Clark and his 1,200 players find dealing with Manfred painful.

Back in the day, players played largely for the love of the game and owners took advantage. All that changed in 1966 when Don Drysdale, a righty pitching stud who owned the inside of the plate coming off 23-12 1965 season, and his pitching teammate Sandy Coufax, Cy Young award winner and even more dominate at 28-8, did something that had never been done before. Koufax couldn't get the raise he wanted, and Drysdale's wife Ginger suggested the two of them work together to get higher pay. Teaming up work, and Koufax got $125,000, with Drysdale getting $100,000. (Ginger, my tennis partner at the Calabasas Park Tennis Club, and related this story to me one day.)

Shortly after this Marvin Miller put the MLBPA on the map, founding the organization in 1966. (He hung around until 1983!) I once had a brief encounter with Marvin. I had developed animated sports trading card flip books I'd named "Thumbshots" and was looking for licensing rights. Marvin said simply, "Whatever royalty rate you pay the league, I want the same for my players." Now, paying double royalties was a no-no at the time, but was non-negotiable to Marvin. So, we caved and did business.

SANDY KOUFAX   pitcher

Marvin Miller   Executive Director 1966-1983

In 1968, Miller negotiated the first collective bargaining agreement (CBA), raising individual player salaries from $6,000 to $10,000. Fast-forward to more current times, and in 2019 the average annual player salary was $4.36 million with a minimum of $555,000 per player.

My radical suggestion is to create a new organizational structure. In it, Manfred remains with a new fancy but lesser title and is placed on an equal footing with Clark. Doing this would immediately make the league a players' league like the NBA. A new job description for commissioner would be created with a simple mission: Change the existing culture to recognize that baseball is in trouble, and push monies and time into "saving baseball from itself."

CHAPTER EIGHT

MLB NEEDS TO GO ON OFFENSE BY CHANGING ITS LINEUP CARD

My idea for changing the lineup card is a much easier assignment than if I worked at say MLB corporate headquarters at 245 Park Avenue NYC with the other "empty suits" as internal politics, the rapidly moving calendar and the daily process of putting out fires is external to the pursuit of new strategic initiatives. This season, COVID-19 overwhelmed the country and baseball has suffered along with everyone else. The difference for baseball, however, is the sport was already in trouble. Unfortunately, the total focus on finding a way to play in 2020 has taken priority over all other activities in an "all hands on deck" situation.

Also, in my favor is that I serve only one master — the die-hard baseball fan without a seat at the negotiating table. Further, the 24/7 world fueled by technology, in my opinion, no way renders the game obsolete. Abner Doubleday's design holds up today, as it always has.

LEO DUROCHER & BABE RUTH

MLB however needs to better educate fans on "inside baseball," i.e. how much skill is involved in making the game look so simple.

Leo "The Lip" Durocher, first a shortstop and then later a flamboyant and controversial manager for both Dodgers and Giants, said it best; "Baseball is like church — many attend, few understand." Former infielder Jim Lefebvre also spoke on the subject: "A baseball field must be the most beautiful thing in the world. It's so honest and precise. And we play on it. Every star gets humbled. Every mediocre player has a great moment."

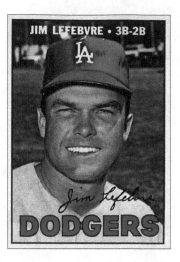

Imagine you were the copywriter for a Madison Avenue NYC-based advertising agency who handled MLB — my dream job, if I had only learned grammar in grade school! *(What the heck is a parallel structure?)* Imagine further you were frustrated by the **game's inability to believe in itself** and wrote a series of defensive-minded headlines to make the point under the umbrella title: "You Can't Be Afraid to Promote the Game." Some might include:

- Come to a baseball game — its shorter now, giving you time to do other things

- Thanks to baseball netting, you can attend a baseball game without fear of becoming seriously injured

- We didn't punish the Astros players to the extent possible, because cheating has always been a part of the game

- National League — a better game because we let pitchers hit

- Robot home plate umpires prove baseball is tech-savvy

- Our players have fewer concussions than football players

- Michael Jordan's slam dunk is more exciting than watching him attempt to hit a baseball

- Baseball's slogan, "The National Pastime," must be good — it's been around for 164 years

- We don't have enough 5-tool players because the tool shed is empty

- Pete Rose Hall of Fame admission would cause the league to encourage gambling for everyone

- Better bet on baseball games because there are so many more of them.

- It's fun watching old, mostly out-of-shape managers sitting in the dugout dressed in player uniforms

- Hate "homer" announcers because they are inclined to be dishonest.

- Base stealing encourages crime

- Baseball games are so long you get more for your money

- Tommy John's surgery was so successful the procedure should be covered under healthcare for all

- Radar gun use is permitted under the second amendment

- Booing the opposing team is unacceptable social behavior

- Bobble heads allow grown-ups to play with dolls

- Baseball wins in the race for most annoying stats — like WAR-Wins Above Replacement

- How can the baseball be juiced if MLB owns Rawlings, the official baseball supplier

- Baseball, more like chess than football; therefore, appealing to the better educated

- COVID-19 mandated baseball season proves fans need not show-up

Don't you think this pretend satirist deserves to be hired?

Contact me with job offers at:

PeretzHoward@gmail.com

CHAPTER NINE

MAKING THE ON-FIELD BASEBALL PRODUCT BETTER

My eleven recommendations for baseball follow a singular thread: recognition of the pre-COVID-19 concerns, the simple diagnostic part, followed by common sense out-of-the-batters-box solutions. Fortunately, the game's problems are in the bottom of the 7th inning, all fans taking a hopeful stretch and singing along in broadcaster Harry Caray-style — it's not the last of the 9th.

Here are my 11 suggestions:

1. GET RID OF THE SLOGAN "NATIONAL PASTIME"

The slogan first appeared in the *New York Sunday Mercury* news 164 years ago in December of 1856. That's before the Civil War! The paper was also the first to report on an actual game in 1853 between the Knickerbockers and Gothams.

Baseball appears willing to "let sleeping dogs lie." The Las Vegas Convention Bureau, by contrast, acted and acted swiftly. They announced at the Grammy Award Ceremony on January 26, 2020, the bureau had changed its successful 2003 slogan, "What happens in Vegas stays in Vegas" to "What happens here **only** happens here." Subtle, smart and naturally woke, well before the statues starting tumbling down.

Back in the 1960s, when I flirted with the corporate identity business, we studied the NYC utility Con Edison. Edison ran a year-in and year-out multi-million-dollar advertising campaign promoting the slogan "Dig we must for a better New York." Research demonstrated that this approach backfired and caused Con Edison to be blamed for every pot hole in New York City; estimated at 300,000 in spring 2016. A new approach went with Con Energy standing for Clean Energy, and it worked!

I suggest replacing the slogan "The National Pastime" with **"America's Ballpark"** which I have trademarked. (Good ideas are rare and worth protecting!) In my opinion, the word past is the killer. Few people care about the past nowadays, especially young people. A high school student interviewed for a NYT Magazine piece in the mid-1980s said, "Why study history? It's all about dead people."

Merriam-Webster defines a ballpark as: "A park or stadium on which ball games such as baseball are played." NFL stadiums, apart from the one-off Lambeau Field home of the Green Bay Packers, are largely oval shaped, tucked away in the suburbs and are void of personality. Amazingly, the New York Giants and the New York Jets play out of the city and out of state in New Jersey.

MLB ballparks, on the other hand, with 24 new parks added since 1989, have a rich feel with distinctive shapes, décor and dimensions, and they are increasingly a part of the urban landscape. Ballparks have been rated for convenience, walkability, and mass transit. Ball Parks at the top of the walkability list are Toronto's Sky Dome, the Cubs' Wrigley Field,

WRIGLEY FIELD

FENWAY PARK

Boston's Fenway Park, San Francisco's AT&T Park and Tigers Comerica Field. Honorable mention went to Cleveland, Baltimore, Denver and Houston. Yankee Stadium, "The Cathedral of Baseball," is mass transit accessible and also scored highly.

YANKEE STADIUM

A change in the slogan is really a huge deal and will be fought every step of the way. Change to the Holy Grail is difficult to accept, but why go down with the Titanic? Executed properly, and having seen this up close, a new slogan can generate positive energy throughout the management pyramid from commissioner to the ball boy/girl.

Of interest to serious baseball fans is a 2019 book about ballpark design titled *Ballpark: Baseball in the American City* by Pulitzer Prize winning architectural critic Paul Goldberger.

2. HITTING A BASEBALL IS THE MOST DIFFICULT TASK IN SPORTS

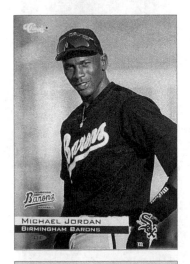

MICHAEL JORDAN
BIRMINGHAM BARONS

RAY CHAPMAN
S. S.—Cleveland Americans
29

Why does baseball keep this difficulty a secret? Just ask Michael Jordan. He would tell you that flying through the air for a foul line takeoff slam dunk is much easier than hitting a curve ball. Jordan batted just .202 for the White Sox Double- A affiliate Birmingham Barons. (Jordan's attempt at baseball was a promise he made to his late dad.)

Baseball is not a game for sissies. Back on August 17, 1920 the Indians' Ray Chapman was beaned by a pitch from the Yankees' Carl Mays and died immediately. His is the only on field death in the history of the game. Finally, batting helmets appeared in 1941 and became mandatory in 1971.

Fastballs thrown off a mound elevated 10" above the playing surface from a distance of 60'6" at 90+ mph by say a Roger Clemens or Nolan Ryan means the hitter must react in 150 milliseconds to hit the ball. It's no wonder the best hitters are successful just 30% of the time.

I had a chance once to see up close and personal a fastball thrown by the pitcher with intent to send a telegram to the hitter. It was in an exhibition contest at Dodger Stadium before the regular game between the Hollywood Stars and retired Dodgers. I was there as the representative of the cre-

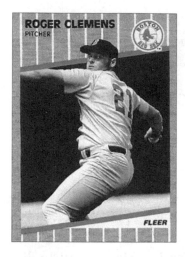

ators of H. R. Pufnstuf, a kid's television series. I dressed but didn't play. The self-appointed Captain of our team, who elected to bat himself first but couldn't hit a lick, was the late comedian Jerry Lewis, known for his antics and shtick.

At the top of the first, Lewis was at bat and Drysdale was on the hill. Lewis would not quit showing-up Drysdale, who finally had enough. He reared back and flattened Lewis, who came up looking horrified. Drysdale had accomplished his objective; Lewis happily shut up for the rest of the evening.

Even though Lewis proved himself to be irritating, it should, however, be noted that he raised millions of dollars for Muscular Dystrophy hosting the MDA Labor Day Telethon from 1968-2010.

In 1941 Red Sox player Ted Williams, "The Splendid Splinter," was the last to hit .400-.406. The .400 hit club numbers 35 players, 19 of whom played in the 1880s. Eight hitters have had a legitimate shot at .400 since Williams. Tony Gwynn of the Padres, a singles hitter, in a shortened season came the closest in 2004 at .394.

CHARLES BARKLEY

To prove inherent difficulty of smacking a baseball, I suggest sending a fleet of traveling batting cages throughout the country, focusing on celebrity contestants. After seeing his golf swing, I would start with the likable and willing Sir Charles Barkley "the Round Mound of Rebound." Staff cages with hitting instructors, publish scores, and provide safety helmets, and MLB authenticated balls and bats. The Houston Astros within their stadium are one of many clubs that promote batting cage events as part of a group special events promotion.

Importantly, batting cages would also be utilized outside of ballparks, before selected games with an emphasis against youngsters and over-aged one-time ex-jocks trying to impress their companions. Each pitching machine would be named after a famous pitcher with ball speed adjusted accordingly from fireball lefty Randy Johnson to control RHP Greg Maddux.

Note: Please no March or November games. Hitting a baseball in cold nasty weather adds an extra degree of difficulty not needed.

3 . BASEBALL HAS ITS OWN DISTINCT VERSION OF *MANO A MANO*

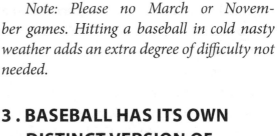

The term *mano a mano* is most often associated with boxing — two tough guys alone in the ring trying to kill each other. I became a big fight fan from the time my dad took me to the local fight club at St. Nicholas Arena in NYC to see a full card of prize fighting. (I was under-aged at the time.) We had a gentleman's bet on every one of the undercard fights.

My dad, again my hero, had chest hair and I assumed such hair was a sign of strength. I had my choice of which fighter to bet on, and I took the guy with the most chest hair—I lost every bet.

There are so many classic encounters in the "Squared Circle" in my memory vault: "Thrilla in Manilla," "Rumble in the Jungle," "Valentine's Day Massacre", the "Bite Fight," Tommy "Hitman" Hearns vs. "Marvelous" Marvin Hagler, Roberto Duran ("No-Mas") vs. Sugar Ray Leonard, Gatti vs. Ward, Yvon Durelle vs. "The Old Mongoose" Archie Moore, Zale vs. Graziano, Joe Louis "The Brown Bomber" vs. "Jersey" Joe Walcott, Pryor vs. Arguello, Chavez vs. Taylor, and most recently, the first fight between Fury and Wilder. (I also can't really ignore Sylvester Stallone as "Rocky.")

JAKE LaMOTTA

Baseball, unlike all other team sports, features *mano a mano* duels with the staging of a battle between an ace pitcher and a home run slugger. Pitchers have long dominated hitters, but the headlines apart from no-hitters and perfect games, go to the hitters whose home runs in the post season decided the outcome: Kirk Gibson, Bill Mazeroski, Joe Carter, Bobby Thomson, Aaron Boone, George Brett, Travis Ishikawa, Derek Jeter, Howie Kendrick, Raul Ibanez, Brandon Belt, Mark Teixeira, Robin Ventura, "Big Papi" David Ortiz, Chris Burke, Max Muncy, Carlton Fisk, Kirby

MUHAMMAD ALI

Puckett, Eddie Matthews, Chris Chambliss, Ozzie Smith, Jose Atuve, Lenny Dykstra, Scott Podsednik," Magglio "Ordonez, Ted Williams (All-

Star Game), and Reggie Jackson (3 home runs—"Mr. October"), among others.

Perfection on the mound has been achieved 23 times. None of them is more famous than Don Larsen's perfect game on October 8, 1956 against the Dodgers. This is the only time a pitcher pitched a perfect game in the World Series.

No-hitters are far more abundant — 260 in the modern era: Nolan Ryan-7, Sandy Koufax-4, and Justin Verlander and Cy Young three each. Johnny Vander Meer for the Reds amazingly threw two no-hitters in back-to-back July 1938 starts.

I, like most fans, treasure the ones I see in person. I had the good fortune to see the Yankees Allie "The Chief" Reynolds throw his second career no-hitter on September 28, 1951, the last day of the regular season. I had played hooky from school when hooky was not tolerated.

If the Yankees defeated the Red Sox in game one of the doubleheader and then tied in the second game, they would win the AL pennant. Reynolds was coasting to victory and was one out away from the no-no when up stepped Ted Williams, the greatest left-handed hitter/slugger of all-time. Williams popped-up behind the plate, Yogi Berra turned, disposed of his mask for the easy catch but the ball fell out of his glove for an error. Reynolds gave Berra words of encouragement and on the following pitch, and Williams did the same thing but this time Yogi squeezed the ball. The Yankees would win game two and then the World Series.

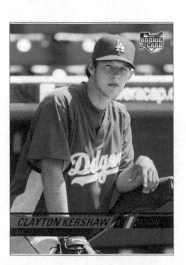

Pitchers, like NFL quarterbacks and NBA point guards, are the most important athletes on the field. These include top closers like Mariano "Sandman" Rivera, Trevor

Hoffman and Lee Smith; strikeout leaders Nolan Ryan, Randy Johnson, Roger Clemens, Steve Carlton; and the Dual Hardware Elite, pitchers winning both the Cy Young Award and MVP in the same year—Clayton Kershaw, Dennis Eckersley and Roger Clemens.

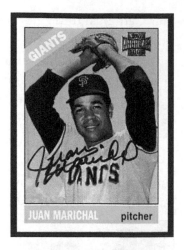

Confrontations between hitters and pitchers are legendary, but in the interest of brevity, I call your attention to two such moments that tower above the rest. On August 22, 1965 the Giants and Dodgers were at it again and all hell broke out when Juan Marichal went after Dodgers shortstop Maury Wills. Both benches erupted, resulting in the ugliest moment in the history of the game. Marichal clubbed Dodgers catcher John Roseboro over the head with a bat, and Willie Mays became the peacemaker.

In a very different moment, also in a game between heated rivals, George Brett homered once again off "Goose" Gossage, but out came Yankees skipper Billy "The Kid" Martin. Martin was a tough kid from

Oakland, and had boxed as an amateur and once almost came to blows with "Mr. October" Reggie Jackson, when he took Reggie out of the game for loafing after a fly ball in right field.

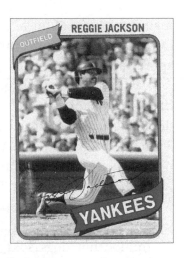

Tradition was, the manager and player — especially a star — would sort things out in the dugout. But Martin, forever the fighter, sent Paul Blair out immediately to replace Jackson, causing sparks to fly. This time, Martin grabbed Brett's bat as he rounded the bases, claiming the pine tar on the bat exceeded 18." He was correct, and Brett went from a home run to an out. He came flying out of the dugout to protest, and he was ejected.

Later, the home run was allowed, but the emotional damage had been done. This event, forever referred to as "The Pine Tar Incident," occurred on July 24, 1983.

MLB would be smart to showcase the best of these mano a mano moments and dub them: The Greatest Bouts in MLB History"

4. BEST FAN GIVEAWAY: SINGLE ADMISSION DAYTIME TWIN BILL WITH A FOOD KICKER

Before the first night game was played at Cincinnati's Crosley Field on May 24, 1935, William Wrigley, former Cubs owner, believed night baseball would be a passing fad. Today, baseball games played during the day are a rarity and have declined to just 10% of games played. Fewer than five teams play less than 100 games under the lights.

The single admission daytime doubleheader, once an industry staple, is even rarer. In 1943, the Chicago White Sox played a record 44 single admission doubleheaders. The argument against doubleheaders is predictable: maximizing revenue, longer duration of games, five man pitching rotation rather than four and not over using relief pitchers, especially stud closers. Ignored are the needs of fans who are looking for an affordable all-day outing. The average cost for a family of four attending a baseball game is $212, with the cost being much higher in major markets. More baseball at a lower cost is the truest form of fan appreciation,

My approach would be to have three mandatory holiday daytime doubleheaders: Memorial Day, July 4th, and Labor Day. As an added bonus, the cost for Ball Park Franks would be rolled back to 1958 prices, when the brand was first popularized by the Detroit Tigers. There are 22 million hot dogs sold yearly at ballparks. America is blessed to have the World's #1 competitive eater as rated by Major League Eating, Joey

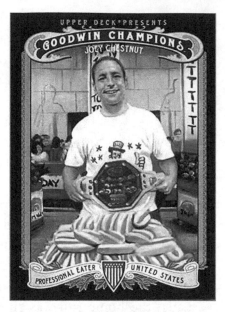

Chestnut. Chestnut holds the record of 69 dogs and buns in ten minutes.

5. PACE OF PLAY NOT A SERIOUS PROBLEM

Since 2015, MLB has made it a priority to reduce the length of a typical nine inning contest. Several rule changes are being made and have been made that make sense and will achieve the desired outcome. In 2005, the average length of a nine-inning game was two hours and 45 minutes. Today, game length exceeds three hours.

MLB is naïve to think shortening the game by 15 minutes will result in significant dividends. I've never watched a fan leave a Yankees vs. Red Sox game, average length three hours and 41 minutes, where managers over-managed and the hitters go long in to the count.

It reminds me of a recent chat I had with a classic TMC movie-goer discussing the virtues of higher-priced stadium seating. He emphatically said he would rather see Gone with the Wind at nearly four hours in length or the nine-hour Godfather Trilogy than a "crappy" short movie in a plush stadium seat.

A startling statistic is the NFL's average game length is three hours, with only 11 minutes of actual action — no one seems to be complaining about that. NFL games are longer as a result of more injuries, extensive replay use, two challenges per coach per game, incomplete passing plays that stop the clock, concussion on-field mandated stoppages, and more commercials. Perhaps MLB has listened to too many GEICO spots, i.e. "**15 minutes** could save you 15% or more..."

6. FREE AUTOGRAPH ENCOURAGEMENT

Players are highly programmed by their greedy agents, among others, to charge for their autographs. In a fan-friendly world, active players should be seen on highlight reels signing their John Hancock's for adoring fans, rather than viewing signing autographs as a painful requirement. Fans are, after all, the ones that pay their salaries.

Back in 1999, while working with former NYC-based sports marketing agency NMG, which was handling publicity for my first book *It Ain't Over 'Til The Fat Lady Sings,* I discovered one of their major playing clients was MLBPA. Their assignment for this client was to escort players to trading card shows for a mandatory signing activity.

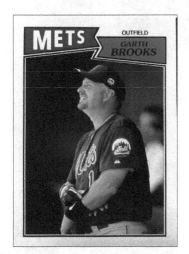

MLB should take a leadership position by making this simple declaration: "We encourage every team and its players to enjoy signing free autographs, with special emphasis on young fans, to support all league-sanctioned activities, including pre-game autograph booths, spring training games in Florida and Arizona, fanfest styled events, and trading card shows."

A great example of this attitude would be Singer/songwriter and Country music superstar Garth Brooks who briefly had a fling at playing baseball. On June 11, 1996, Brooks hosted a spectacular free autograph experience during Fan Fest at the Tennessee State Fair. He set up an unannounced makeshift tent where he greeted his faithful fans and signed autographs for 23 straight hours. He continued signing until the last fan in line happily walked away with his autograph.

7. FULL PRESS TO IDENTIFY, AND SELECT THE "FIVE TOOL PLAYER"

MIKE TROUT   OF

A five-tool player is one who hits for exit velocity and power, with fielding rate efficiency and ability to throw and run. In a sports landscape dominated by stars, only 1.6%, or just six players, possessed this skill set in 2019: Mike Trout, "Mookie" Betts, Jose Ramirez, Alex Bregman, Aaron Hicks, and Ronald Acuna, Jr. They are no Mickey Mantle, Roberto Clemente, Frank Robinson or Willie Mays.

ROBERTO CLEMENTE   outfield PITTSBURGH PIRATES

Kyler Murray, the 2018 Heisman Trophy winner at quarterback out of Oklahoma, had five tool potential but chose the NFL's Arizona Cardinals instead. Murray won the NFL 2019 Offensive Rookie of the Year award. Murray passed on a first of its kind guaranteed baseball signing offer with the Oakland A's backed by MLB rule bending — they were all-in, but chalk up another win for the NFL. The problem was not getting to Murray early enough in his baseball career.

ROOKIE GRIDIRON KINGS

CARDINALS

KYLER MURRAY

The solution would be to establish a Five Tool Academy for youngsters exhibiting the necessary potential. These future stars would be evaluated beginning in Little League, and invited to spend summers at the academy where the teaching, facilities, encouragement from baseball royalty, and guidance would be second to none. Graduates of the academy would, in many ways, be treated like high school basketball players named to the McDonald's All-American team.

The academy graduates would have a separate, fast ticket to "The Show," avoiding all of the traditional painful steps in the process, including the yearly draft, Cape Cod-styled summer leagues, college scholarships, and low minor league signings. A sponsor/partnership arrangement would be natural with The Home Depot, Lowe's Home Improvement and Ace Hardware at the obvious top of the list. (Even yours truly could make this naming rights' sale and I would be thrilled to take the commission.)

Attracting African-American youth must be a priority, ala "Black Lives Matter." On this issue, MLB participation by this group has dropped significantly over the years. In 1981, African-Americans represented 18.7% of players, but in 2017 participation had declined to 6.7% in spite of well-intended efforts from the likes of "Hammerin' Hank Aaron. By contrast, the NBA and NFL both have high percentages of African-American athletes; the NBA at 74% and in the NFL at 68%.

Importantly, "heightism" is a think. A 1971 study by sociologist Saul Feldman proves taller people get preference in the workplace. Average male adult height in America is 5'9" while in the NBA it is 6'7", combined with a 6'10" wingspan makes for a high bar for entry. In the NFL, average weight is more significant — 6'2" in height, but 246 lbs. Baseball comes in at 6'2" and 207 pounds, though both height and weight are less significant. Witness all-stars like the Astros 5'6" shortstop Jose Altuve.

8. "HOMER" ANNOUNCERS TO BE OUTRAGEOUS AND PARTISAN

The fans/listeners want someone in the booth who roots for their team — living and dying with every win and loss — not the velvety smooth types like golf's gifted Jim Nantz. A homer announcer is defined as "an announcer who intention- ally plays down the accomplishments of the visiting team in an effort to play-up the home team's accomplishments." In other words, they're colorful but not necessarily truthful.

Ideally a "homer" could be rotated to the Major League Baseball Game of the Week (GOTW). My personal favorites are: Hawk Harrelson's "hawkisms" like sacks packed with Sox;" Ron Santo "the single biggest Cubs fan of all time;" John Sterling, "theeeeeee Yankees win;" Harry Caray who popularized "Take me out to the ballgame" (7th inning stretch) and the "Gunner- isms" from Bob Prince. Vin Scully, a fellow Bronx native and the voice of the Dodgers for 67 years, also qualifies but with an asterisk. He was a one of-a-kind velvety smooth

"homer" made this astute statement about the difference between foot- ball and baseball: **"Football is to baseball as blackjack is to bridge."**

9. AN EMPATHETIC "NO" TO ROBOT HOME PLATE UMPIRES

"Perfection is the enemy of the good." In trying to appear technologically hip, the MLB is serious about using Robot Umpires and has tested the concept in the Atlantic League. While I'm mostly in favor of replays, although they sometimes take too long, subjectivity can still enter

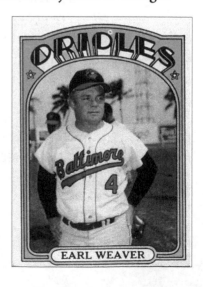

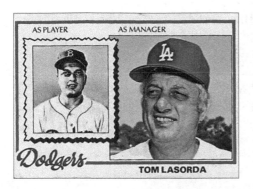

AS PLAYER   AS MANAGER

Dodgers

TOM LASORDA

the picture, but consistency is all that is needed. Some of my favorite baseball moments include managers and umpires arguing balls and strikes, even though the outcome is never changed. Prime culprits who have been ejected include, Earl Weaver, Billy "The Kid" Martin, "Whitey" Herzog, Tommy Lasorda before he lost weight, John Madden, "Sweet" Lou Piniella, Jim Leyland, Ozzie Guillen, and Bobby Valentine.

As an avid fan, I only remember a handful of umpires by name: Art Passarella, Doug Harvey, Al Barlick, and Jocko Conlan. The "ump" puts his masked face into the action and risks the danger of being hit by a foul ball. A robot wouldn't care. Despite the anonymity and the danger, competition to be a big league "ump" is fierce. There are only 68 slots available and there's little turnover, probably due to the average annual salary that ranges from $120,000–$350,000.

This quote from Leo 'The Lip" Durocher totally captures my feeling on the subject: "I never questioned the integrity of the umpire. Their eyesight, yes." (Durocher's eyesight was good enough, however, to land beautiful Hollywood starlet Lorraine Day on February 15, 1948 and he was no Brad Pitt.)

10. DESIGNATED HITTER RULE ADOPTION IS AN EMBARRASSMENT

I'm old school. I was originally opposed to the concept of a designated hitter batting for the pitcher. Back in the day, constructing a lineup was simple: first batter single or walk; second batter, preferably a lefty, moves the runner along by hitting behind him; the third hitter is the best; the fourth is the slugger, the fifth is the RBI guy who's good enough to protect the fourth; batters six through eight aren't very good. The pitcher would ideally make the last out and that was a good thing. At all costs you wanted to avoid the pitcher leading off the next inning.

CHARLIE O. FINLEY

Under the leadership of Charlie O. Finley, the Oakland A's controversial owner, the American League voted 8–4 to adopt the DHR rule on January 3, 1973. The National League gave every indication they would follow, but they did not. They tried once again in 1980 after a strange set of circumstances, but the NL voted no again even though AL attendance demonstrated the popularity of the move, plus the DHR is utilized by most amateur, college and professional leagues.

Pitchers can't hit — they average .109 in the AL and .116 in NL. Pitchers are not paid to hit. They rarely take batting practice and are too valuable to be hit with pitches. The DHR has kept older players, those injured, no longer fleet of foot, and those who are poor fielders in the game.

The overt chaos of the DH differential becomes pronounced during the height of the baseball calendar with inter-league play, the All-Star game and, most critically, the World Series. I can't think of another major sport where the rules are different between divisions, leagues, or conferences.

Three players who were predominately DH have entered the Hall of Fame: Frank Thomas, Edgar Martinez, and Harold Baines. "Big Papi" David Ortiz is waiting in the wings.

If I was selected to be the Commissioner of Baseball, a position I am too old and unqualified to fill, when Manfred took office on January 25, 2015 on my first day I would have issued a Trump-style "executive order" forcing the NL to adopt the DHR the following season. Because of COVID-19, the DHR will be utilized in a condensed 2020 season by all teams, and will require MLBPA approval going forward.

11. REALIGNMENT NECESSARY TO PROMOTE RIVALRIES

With the DHR possibly in place in both leagues, and a condensed 2020 season forcing regional play, smart realignment seems inevitable. "Smart" meaning following regional geography for existing AL and NL teams and swapping teams between leagues to promote natural rivalries. Previously these natural rivalries where reserved for regular season inter-league play which has proven to be successful not impacting the World Series. Please note the Milwaukee Brewers moved from the AL to the NL in 1998, while the Houston Astros from the NL to the AL in 2013.

In my new realignment plan, traditional league separation ignored which the owners will certainly hate until they count their money and fans will love.

- New York Yankees vs. New York Mets

- Washington Nationals vs. Baltimore Orioles

- Miami Marlins vs. Tampa Bay Rays

- Cincinnati Reds vs Cleveland Indians

- Chicago Cubs vs. Chicago White Sox

- St. Louis Cardinals vs. Kansas City Royals

- Oakland A's vs. San Francisco Giants

- Los Angeles Dodgers vs. Los Angeles Angels

See the following page for the proposed AL and NL divisions.

★ AMERICAN ★
★ LEAGUE ★

AL DIVISION 1	AL DIVISION 2	AL DIVISION 3
Boston Red Sox	Washington Nationals*	Toronto Blue Jays
New York Yankees	Baltimore Orioles	Detroit Tigers
New York Mets*	Atlanta Braves*	Cincinnati Reds*
Philadelphia Phillies*	Miami Marlins*	Cleveland Indians
Pittsburgh Pirates*	Tampa Bay Rays	Milwaukee Brewers*

★ NATIONAL ★
★ LEAGUE ★

NL DIVISION 1	NL DIVISION 2	NL DIVISION 3
St. Louis Cardinals	Houston Astros*	Seattle Mariners*
Chicago Cubs	Texas Rangers*	San Francisco Giants
Chicago White Sox*	Arizona Diamondbacks	Oakland A's*
Kansas City Royals*	San Diego Padres	Los Angeles Dodgers
Minnesota Twins*	Colorado Rockies	Los Angeles Angels *

*Indicates proposed league change.

CHAPTER 10

CONCLUSION

The game of baseball is as wonderful as ever; "watching grass grow" is a refreshing, positive change from the pressures of daily life. It's escapism, even though keeping politics out of sports no longer possible (just watch ESPN).

I remember fondly the late sports columnist Jimmy Cannon who said, "Sports is the toy department of life."

I was reminded of the magic of baseball just the other day from, of all people, Timothy Dolan the Archbishop of New York. He was born in St. Louis and is a lifelong Cardinals fan.

TIMOTHY DOLAN

In 2009 he was appointed a Cardinal by the church, putting on his red silk biretta daily as he dressed for church services — once a Cardinal always a Cardinal. He recalls cheering the Cards "Stan the Man Musial" with his dad and grandfather the day he got his 3,000th hit at Chicago's Wrigley Field.

About baseball Dolan says it best: "Baseball is good company."

On the other hand, the business of baseball is having some serious difficulties, because the powers to be are either clueless

stan musial

ST. LOUIS CARDINALS
OUTFIELD-FIRST BASE

as to how to proceed or they do not believe in their gut that baseball can flourish in the 21st Century.

COVID-19 is not the culprit — the 2020 season was heading for disaster anyway, due to the sign stealing scandal, the Commissioner's unfortunate statement about the World Series trophy, and the withdrawal of MLB support for Minor League Baseball, not to mention all the short-term problems facing the sport.

I have been training for a lifetime to write this very personal white paper — **"Saving Baseball from Itself."** I have been following baseball for 72 years. I am glad at age 80 that I believe I'm smart enough to see things clearly and to recommend common sense solutions. I feel confident that this white paper will stand up to scrutiny by baseball die-hards, and the mavens inside the "box" who appear to know everything, but accomplish little.

As sportswriter Red Smith remarked: "Young men have visions, old men have dreams."

Thanks for allowing this Old School Sports Junkie to dream.

Howard G. Peretz
Old School Sports Junkie and published sports author
Cave Creek, Arizona
Mobile: 908-313-2360
Email: peretzhoward@gmail.com

www.Savingbaseball.net

BASEBALL'S
100 GREATEST FINISHES
A Fan's Guide

Howard G. Peretz

© Copyright 2020, Howard G. Peretz

All Rights Reserved.

In accordance with the U.S. Copyright Act of 1976, the scanning, up-loading, and electronic sharing of any part of this book without the permission of the publisher constitute unlawful privacy and theft of the author's intellectual property. If you would like to use material from the book (other than for preview purposes), prior written permission must be obtained by contacting the publisher at the address below. Thank you for your support of the author's rights.

ISBN: 978-1948638-05-0

Cotact the author at: PeretzHoward@gmail.com

Or visit the author's website for more information:

www.SavingBaseball.net

"A baseball game is simply a nervous breakdown divided into nine innings."

—Earl Wilson, legendary gossip columnist, best known for his daily syndicated column "It Happened Last Night"

INTRODUCTION

Of all the sports, baseball has the richest tradition dating to pre-Civil War 1846 contests. The BFI (Baseball Finish Index), an analytical system I pioneered, ranks individual game finishes according to: Magical Moment (1-40 points), Last Play Outcome (1-25 points), Game Importance (1-15 points), Surrounding Environment (1-10 points), and Comeback/Upset (1-10 points).

No event has ever reached a perfect score of 100 points. Bobby Thomson's "The Little Miracle of Coogan's Bluff" comes closest, at 94.5.

In addition to Major League Baseball (MLB) the Index also includes Minor League Baseball (1), College World Series games (2) and Little League Championships (1).

I have researched thousands of games, and what sometimes keeps me up at night is the fear that I may have missed a game. Fortunately, my readers and fans keep me on the straight and narrow.

NOTE: Games played before 1920, in the so-called dead ball era, have been downgraded for the purpose of this list.

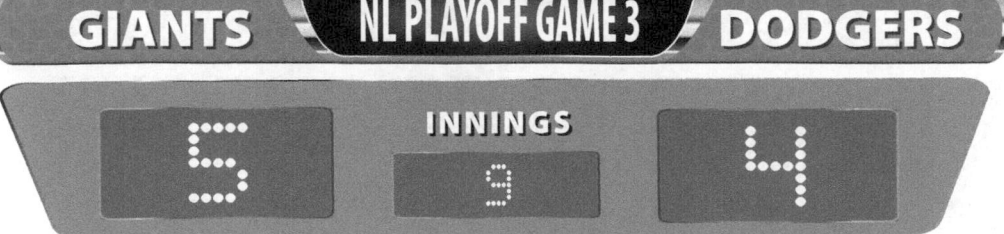

RANKING
1

OCTOBER 3, 1951

GIANTS — NL PLAYOFF GAME 3 — DODGERS

| | INNINGS | |
| 5 | 9 | 4 |

THE MIRACLE OF COOGAN'S BLUFF

With 1 out in the bottom of the 9th, Bobby "The Flying Scot" Thomson's 3-run homerun off reliever Ralph Branca, who was wearing unlucky #13, decided the NL pennant. Dodgers skipper Charlie Dressen had pronounced the Giants dead after a 3-game sweep at Ebbets Field on August 10, increasing their lead to 12-1/2 games over their bitter crosstown rivals. Giants 'homer' announcer Russ Hodges' famous broadcast call memorialized the moment: "The Giants win the pennant! The Giants win the pennant!"

BOBBY THOMSON

1

WISH MY DAD HAD BEEN ALIVE TO SEE IT

Bill "Maz" Mazeroski, Pirates HOF second sacker, hit a walk-off homerun in the bottom of the 9th while Yankees leftfielder Yogi Berra could only turn and watch. The key inning was the bottom of the 8th, when the Pirates scored 5 runs after a potential double play took a weird bounce and hit Yankees shortstop Tony Kubek in the larynx. The Yankees outhit and outpitched the Pirates in the Series, but lost every close game.

CUBS   **WORLD SERIES-GAME 7**   **INDIANS**

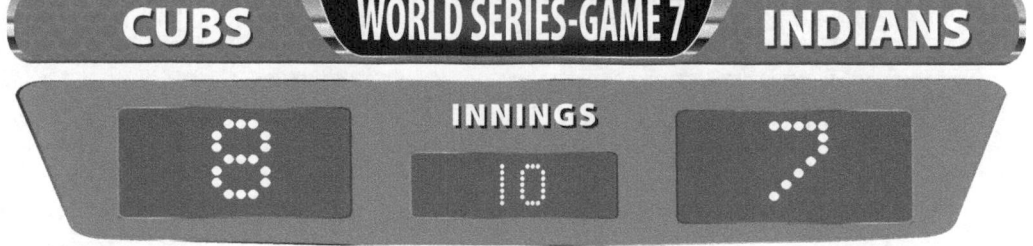

INNINGS

8   10   7

LOVEABLE LOSERS WIN

The Cubs won back to back World Series championships in 1907 and 1908, but failed to win again until this 2016 game. This losing streak is partially attributed to the "Curse of the Billy Goat." In 1945, Tavern owner William Sianis cursed the team when he wasn't allowed into a game with his pet goat. This curse lasted 71 years, from 1945-2016.

Thousands of Cub fans traveled to Cleveland for the 2016 game, completely overwhelming the home crowd. The Cubs were comfortably ahead 5-1 with lefty flame thrower Aroldis Chapman on the mound, when Raja Davis hit a 2-run blast that tied the game in the bottom of the 8th. Ben Zobrist, Series MVP, had the deciding hit in the top of the 10th.

Credit for the Cubs' turnaround goes to GM Theo Epstein, who had previously accomplished the same task with the Boston Red Sox.

ARENA BASEBALL ARRIVES

ALEX BREGMAN

This slugfest that saw 7 homeruns, helped to fuel controversy juiced baseballs. The anticipated pitching duel between Cy Young winners Dallas Keuchel (Astros) and Clayton Kershaw (Dodgers) never materialized. Astros Alex Bregman's single scored pinch runner Derek Fisher in the bottom of the 10th for the win. The game lasted 5 hours and 47-minutes!

BASEBALL TRIVIA

• *On January 13, 2020 an investigation by MLB revealed the Astros were sign-stealing during the 2017 and 2018 seasons.*

CARDINALS — WORLD SERIES-GAME 6 — RANGERS

	INNINGS	
10	11	9

ONE STRIKE AWAY, TWICE

The Cardinals trailed 7-4 after seven innings. It was looking like they were facing elimination, when they twice found themselves down to their final out and their final strike. But they battled back, and came storming back to tie the game both times.

It appeared that Rangers troubled homerun hitter Josh Hamilton had won the game with a 2-run shot in the top of the 10th. However, it was not to be, as Lance Bergman's single tied the game in the bottom of the 10th. The Cardinals

rallied in the bottom of the 11th, when David Freese connected on a full-count pitch from Rangers right-hander Mark Lowe. (Freeze also tied the game with a 2-run single in the bottom of the 9th).

BUCKNER BOOTS THE BALL

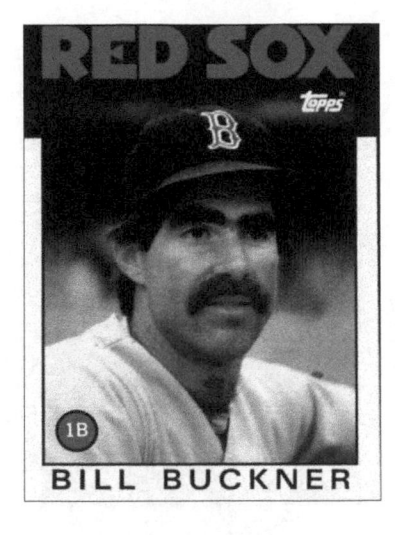

BILL BUCKNER

The Red Sox were one strike away from winning their first championship since 1918 with a lead of 5-3, but the Mets won after overcoming a deficit of two runs with two outs and no one on base in the bottom of the 10th inning. Sox relief pitcher and control specialist Bob Stanley uncorked a wild pitch allowing Ray Knight to reach third. The winning run was scored after a routine ground ball hit by the Mets "Mookie" Wilson went under the glove and between the legs of the Sox first baseman Bill Buckner, allowing Knight to score and the Mets to have a come-from-behind-win.

I'm sure Sox Manager John McNamara regrets to this day that he left Buckner in the game for defensive purposes rather than replacing him with Dave Stapleton.

THE CURSE OF THE BAMBINO

AARON BOONE
Third Base • YANKEES®

Babe "The Bambino" Ruth was traded on December 26, 1919 from Boston to New York, where "The Curse of the Bambino" continued. Boston, which led 4-0 and then 5-2, had Pedro Martinez on the hill in the 8th when the Yankees tied the score. Sox Manager Grady Little went to the mound to remove the Hall of Famer and three-time Cy Young Award winner, but Martinez insisted on staying in the game.

The Yankees won in the 11th when Aaron Boone, who entered the game as a pinch runner, hit Tim Wakefield's first knuckle ball into the left field stands.

On the day following the game, Red Sox Manager Grady Little was fired, and on December 4, 2017 Aaron Boone was named the Yankee's skipper.

BASEBALL TRIVIA

• *Aaron's brother Brett was in the booth as a guest announcer for this game.*

7

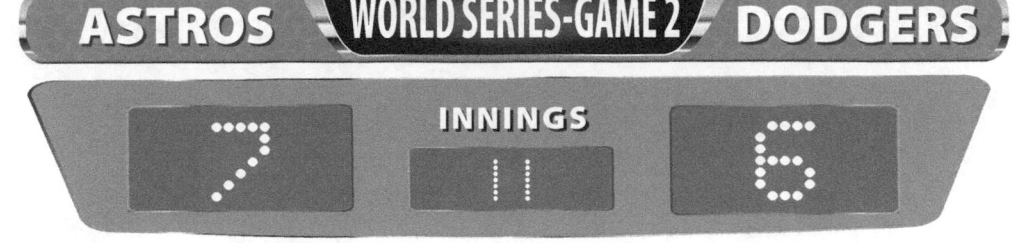

ASTROS   WORLD SERIES-GAME 2   DODGERS

INNINGS

7   11   6

ASTROS FIRST WORLD SERIES WIN

GEORGE SPRINGER
OUTFIELDER

The Astros, founded in 1962, were looking for their first World Series win and sent ace Justin Verlander to the mound. Verlander with three no-hitters to his credit left after 6-innings, with the Astros trailing 3-1. He gave up just 2 hits, but both were homeruns.

Dodgers All-Star closer Kenley Jansen couldn't quite close the deal, allowing a tying homerun in the 9th to Marwin Gonzalez. The Astros went ahead in the top of the 10th but the Dodgers Yasiel Puig homered to send the contest in to the 11th inning.

George Springer's 2-run blast off reliever Brandon McCarthy turned out to be the game winner.

BLUE JAYS

WORLD SERIES–GAME 6

PHILLIES

INNINGS

8   11   6

THE WILD THING'S BLOWN SAVE

The Blue Jays were trailing 6–5 in the bottom of the 9th when Joe Carter hit a three-run home for the win. Phillies closer Mitch "The Wild Thing" Williams, had control problems and was the victim of Carter's walk-off shot.

This was only the second Series in history concluded by such a home run - the first was in 1960 (see ranking #2).

BASEBALL TRIVIA

• *Blue Jays broadcaster coined the famous phrase "Touch 'em all Joe" for Carter's amazing play.*

• *"The Wild Thing" got his nickname from the 1993 film* Major League. *He even had the same jersey number as the character in the movie — #99.*

THE NATURAL

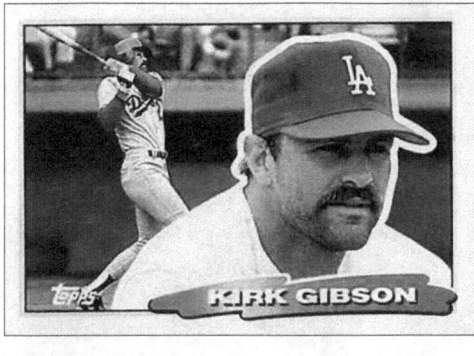

Mike Davis reached on a walk, setting the stage for Kirk Gibson, who wasn't expected to play due to injuries a left hamstring strain and a sprained medial collateral ligament in his right knee. Gibson pinch-hit a 2-out, walk-off homerun off A's HOF All-Star closer Dennis Eckersley.

Vin Scully, legendary Dodgers broadcaster, who recently retired after 67 years, had reported Gibson was not in uniform at the start of the game.

Gibson's role in this game reminds me of the 1984 movie *The Natural* where a baseball player who comes out of nowhere takes the baseball world by storm, launching towering home run with his seemingly magic bat.

BASEBALL TRIVIA

• *Gibson was named National League MVP. He also played football at Michigan State.*

RED SOX **WORLD SERIES-GAME 6** REDS

INNINGS

7 12 6

FISK AND THE FOUL POLE

Red Sox player Bernie Carbo, a former Cincinnati player, hit a 3-run pinch hit homerun in the bottom of the 8th off Pat Darcy to tie the game. Carbo trash-talked in a fun way to ex-teammate Pete Rose as he rounded the bases.

In the 12th inning, HOF All-Star catcher Carlton "Pudge" Fisk hit the most famous home run of his career. His blast was inside the left field foul pole above the Green Monster. Fisk was rooting for the ball to "stay fair" and waving his arms as he watched it fly.

The Fisk homerun won the game and tied the Series at three games each.

BASEBALL TRIVIA

• *Fisk had 371 career homeruns.*

• *In a 2010 ESPN interview Carbo revealed that when he came to bat during this game he had been using both drugs and alcohol.*

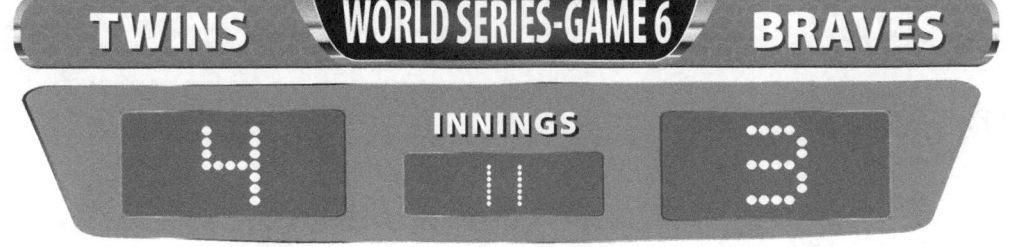

TWINS   WORLD SERIES-GAME 6   BRAVES

INNINGS

4   11   3

"AND WE'LL SEE YOU TOMORROW NIGHT"

FLEER 91

KIRBY
PUCKETT

HOF Twins centerfielder Kirby Puckett, who spent his entire career with the club, hit a walk-off homerun off Charlie Leibrandt, forcing a game seven. Reportedly Puckett had planned to bunt for a base hit, but teammate Chili Davis, the on-deck batter, said, "Bunt my ass."

The moment was captured by sportscaster Jack Buck's call: "And we'll see you tomorrow night!"

BASEBALL TRIVIA

• *Puckett rounding second base after this home run is represented in statue form in front of the Twins ballpark, Target Center.*

"BOSTON STRONG"

Red Sox future Hall of Famer David "Big Papi" Ortiz, who had 14 seasons with the team, seized the moment once again by lacing a grand slam home run in the bottom of the 8th to tie the game. Tigers' outfielder and gold glove winner Torii Hunter jumped for the ball before crashing over the fence and disappearing in to the bullpen.

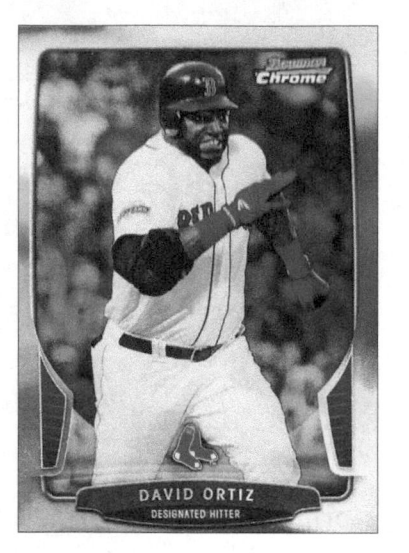

DAVID ORTIZ
DESIGNATED HITTER

Red Sox bullpen cop and Boston Police Officer Steve Hogan, a member of Boston's finest, raised the ball, becoming an instant hero. In the bottom of the 9th, Jarrod Saltalamacchia's hit brought home Johnny Gomes for the winning run.

BASEBALL TRIVIA

• *Boston Marathon bombing earlier in the year on April 15 resulted in the saying "Boston Strong."*

13

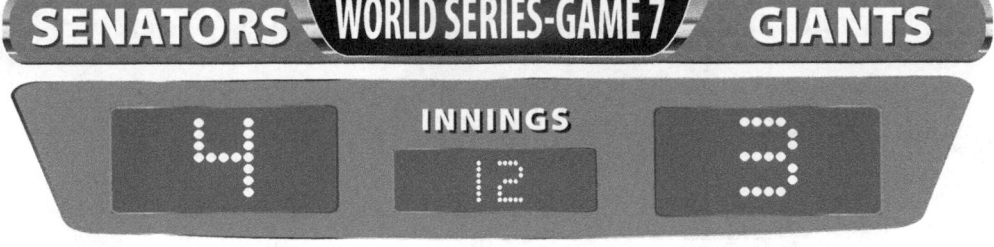

RANKING
14
OCTOBER 10, 1924
SENATORS — WORLD SERIES-GAME 7 — GIANTS

INNINGS

4   12   3

PEBBLES HIT TWICE

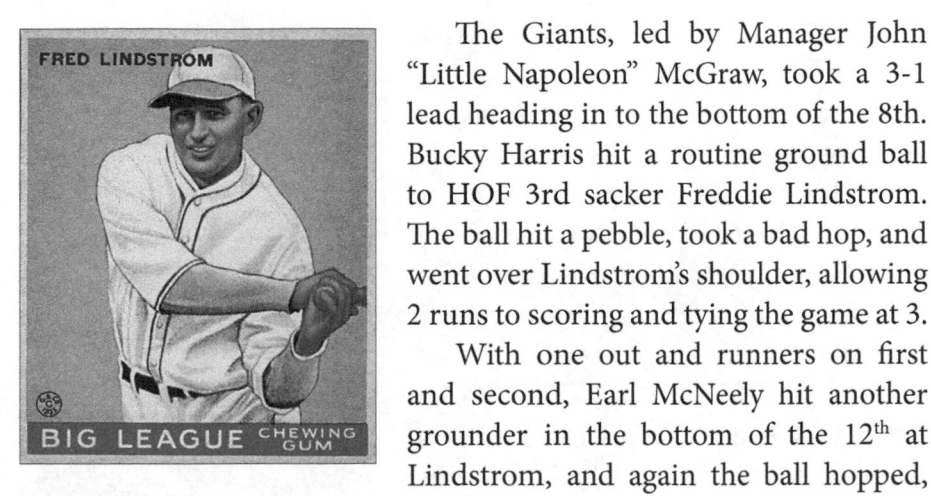

FRED LINDSTROM

BIG LEAGUE CHEWING GUM

The Giants, led by Manager John "Little Napoleon" McGraw, took a 3-1 lead heading in to the bottom of the 8th. Bucky Harris hit a routine ground ball to HOF 3rd sacker Freddie Lindstrom. The ball hit a pebble, took a bad hop, and went over Lindstrom's shoulder, allowing 2 runs to scoring and tying the game at 3.

With one out and runners on first and second, Earl McNeely hit another grounder in the bottom of the 12th at Lindstrom, and again the ball hopped, scoring Muddy Ruel with the Series-winning run. Legend had it that the same pebble was hit twice.

BASEBALL TRIVIA

• *This was Walter "Big Train" Johnson, who is second to Cy Young in total games won (417), won his only World Series game win in relief.*

• *Bucky Harris became the Senator's skipper later that year at the age of 27.*

• *In 1961, the hapless Senators moved to the Twin Cities where they became the Minnesota Twins.*

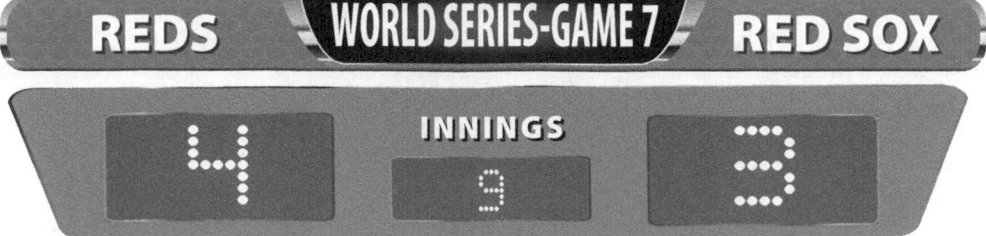

FIRST TIME

After a 34-year hiatus, the Reds won the Series, going down to the 9th inning of game seven — but it was not easy. The unsung hero for the Reds was their bullpen, throwing five scoreless innings. Boston led 3–0 after 3 innings at Fenway.

After a botched double play ball, HOF Tony Perez's 2-run shot over the Green Monster brought the Reds to within one run. HOF Pete Rose's RBI single evened the score in the bottom of the 7th.

In the 9th, Ken Griffey Sr. scored the go-ahead run after a lead-off walk, as HOF Joe Morgan reached out, hitting a bloop single for the winning run.

ESPN named the 1975 Series the "Greatest World Series Ever".

BASEBALL TRIVIA

• *When baseball fans argue about which team is the greatest of all time, inevitably, the 1976 "Big Red Machine" is matched against the 1927 New York Yankees.*

RANKING
16
JULY 8, 1941
ALL-STAR GAME
AL   NL
INNINGS
7   9   5

TED WILLIAMS FAVORITE HIT

"TED" WILLIAMS

This ninth playing of the All-Star game the greatest in history. It took place at a time when the All Star game was played for bragging rights, not just an exhibition.

The hero of the game, played at Detroit's Briggs Stadium, was Boston Red Sox Ted "Splendid Splinter" Williams. With the NL leading 5–4, with two outs in the bottom of the 9th inning, and Joe Gordon and Joe DiMaggio of the New York Yankees on base; Ted Williams hit a walk-off 3-run home run off of Claude Passeau of the Chicago Cubs to win it for the AL.

BASEBALL TRIVIA

• *Williams had a career .344 batting average and 521 homeruns.*

• *In 1941, Williams hit .406 and was the last hitter to break that barrier.*

• *Williams missed five years on the ball field due to serving as an ace fighter pilot in both World War II and the Korean War.*

• *Also in 1941, Joe DiMaggio hit in 56 consecutive games and beat out Williams for the AL MVP.*

ARIZONA'S ONLY PRO SPORTS VICTORY

The Diamondbacks won with superb pitching from starters HOF Randy "The Big Unit" Johnson and Curt Schilling Co-MVP's holding the four-time defending champion Yankees to a Series batting average of .183, the lowest on record for a seven-game series.

Luis Gonzalez • OF

ARIZONA DIAMONDBACKS

The Yankees, however, led by 1-run heading to the bottom of the 9th with the best closer in the game's history, 652 saves to his credit, "The Sandman" Mariano Rivera on the hill for a 2-inning save. It was not to be. In the 8th Tony Womack's double scored one. In the 9th after Yankees 3rd sacker Scott Brosius failed to throw to first on a double play ball, with the bases loaded and the infield in, Luis "Gonzo" Gonzalez single to score Jay Bell for the victory.

BASEBALL TRIVIA

• *The 2001 World Series was played in the shadow of the 9/11 terrorist bombing of the Twin Towers in NYC.*

ROYALS   ALWC PLAY-IN GAME   OAKLAND A's

INNINGS

9   12   8

"KANSAS CITY HERE I COME"

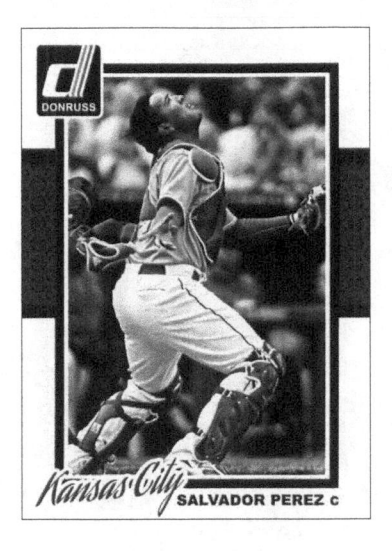

SALVADOR PEREZ c

The Oakland A's were well on their way to winning this play-in game, leading 7-3 entering the 8th behind ace John Lester. Lester is 85-1 in his career with a 4-run lead. Lester along with Adam Dunn and Johnny Gomes, who was traded to the A's in mid-season as Billy Beane of "Money Ball" Fame doubled down.

The Royals ran wild, with 7-stolen bases in the contest. Royals Jarred Dyson scored the tying run in the bottom of the 9th, after swiping third. The win came in the 12th on a single by Salvatore Perez.

BASEBALL TRIVIA

• *The Royals led the majors that year with 153 stolen bases.*

• *Many Royals fans considered this "The Best Game Ever" because of the team's incredible 4-run comeback.*

• *"Kansas City Here I Come" is a song by Lieber and Stoller.*

RED SOX   ALCS GAME FOUR   YANKEES

6   INNINGS   4

12

"CURSE OF THE BAMBINO" FINALLY OVER

DAVID ORTIZ

The Yankees had won the first 3 games of the series, including a 19–8 game three shellacking that included 22 hits and 4 home runs.

Things looked bleak for the Red Sox, since no team had ever come back from a 3-0 deficit before, and because the Red Sox hadn't won a championship in 86-years due to "the curse." The Yankees took a 1-run lead in to the 9th behind Mariano Rivera going for the save and now in his second inning of relief.

In the 9th Kevin Millar walked, followed by a stolen base to pinch-runner Dave Roberts, then a single by Bill Mueller tied the game. In the bottom of the 12th, with Paul Quantrill pitching, a single by Manny Ramirez was followed by a walk-off homerun from David "Big Papi" Ortiz. This was the second walk-off homer for Ortiz in this post season — a first in the history of the game.

Amazingly, Boston would go on to win game 5, 6, and 7 and move on to the World Series, where they defeated the St. Louis Cardinals.

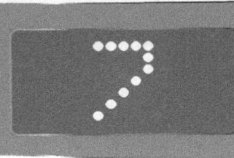 **BRAVES** **WORLD SERIES-GAME 4** **YANKEES**

 **INNINGS** **10**

7 5

EDDIE MATTHEWS BECOMES COVER BOY

In pivotal game four, the Yankees had tied the contest in the top of the 9th on Elston Howard's 3-run blast with 2-outs. The Yankees went ahead in the top of the 10th on a triple by "Hank the Howitzer" Bauer.

The Braves were down by a run in the bottom of the 10th but rallied to win, after a double by Johnny Logan and a towering 2-run walk-off homerun by Braves HOF 3rd baseman Eddie Matthews.

The Braves would win the Series in 7 games, their first since moving to Milwaukee from Boston.

BASEBALL TRIVIA

• *Howard was the first African-American to play for the Yankees.*

• *Matthews would appear on the first cover of* Sports Illustrated *in 1957.*

CARDINALS — WORLD SERIES-GAME 7 — YANKEES

	INNINGS	
3	9	2

BABE RUTH OUT STEALING

The Cardinals won their first championship when in the bottom of the 9th, with 2-outs and the Yankees down 1 run, Babe Ruth was on first. He took off on his own and was easily gunned out by catcher Bob O'Farrell. This was a dumb move by Ruth, considering the batters behind him were Bob Meusel, Lou Gehrig, Tony Lazzeri, and "Jumpin" Joe Dugan.

The save went to HOF "Old Pete" Grover Cleveland Alexander, who entered the game in the 7th inning. This Series win by the Cardinals was their first championship.

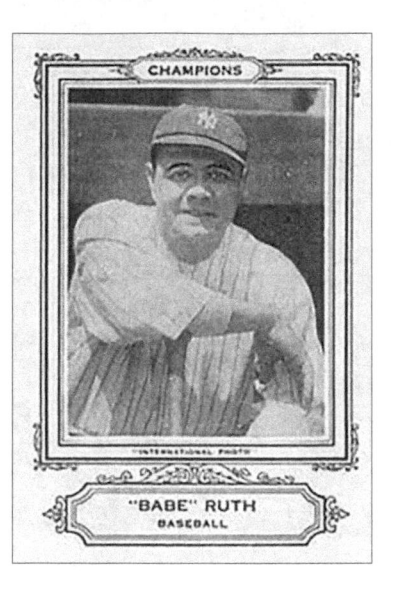

CHAMPIONS

"BABE" RUTH
BASEBALL

BASEBALL TRIVIA

• *Alexander had 373 career wins, tossing complete game victories in games two and six in this Series.*

• *Ruth hit 3-homeruns, in game 4 of this Series. He was the first to do this. He also hit a homerun in game 7.*

• *Ruth hit 714 homeruns in career had a record of 123 steals in 249 attempts.*

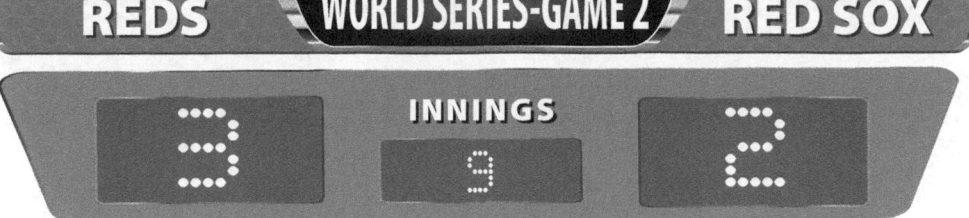

GRIFFEY SR. THE HERO

Red Sox left hander Bill "Spaceman" Lee was throwing a masterpiece against the loaded Reds lineup — one run on four hits through 8 innings. In the top of the 9th, Johnny Bench, arguably best catcher of all time followed by Yogi Berra and Roy Campanella, opened the inning with a double.

Lee left the game and was replaced by closer Dick Drago, who with 2 outs gave up a clutch RBI single to shortstop Dave Concepcion, who promptly stole second.

Ken Griffey Sr. known as a table setter for "The Big Red Machine" doubled to left center for the game winner.

BASEBALL TRIVIA

• *Griffey Sr., is father of celebrated HOF Ken Griffey Jr.*

• *Griffey Sr. had a .296 career batting average, and was a three time All-Star.*

• *He played ball from 1973-1991.*

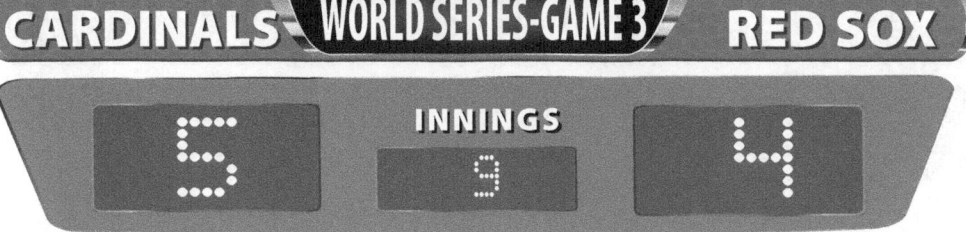

CARDINALS — WORLD SERIES-GAME 3 — RED SOX

| 5 | INNINGS 9 | 4 |

CAN YOU MEASURE INTENT

It all boiled down to one play in the bottom of the 9th. Cards Yadier Molina hit a 1-out single off Sox closer Koji Uehera and moved to third on a double by Allen Craig. Jon Jay then grounded to second sacker Dustin Pedroia, who speared the ball and threw home to catcher Jarred Saltamaacchia, who tagged Molina out.

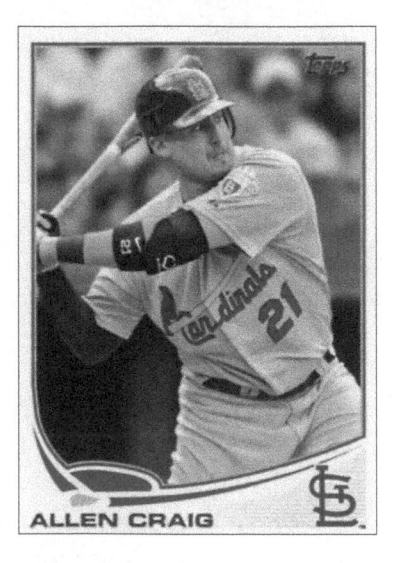

ALLEN CRAIG

On the throw home, Craig went to third. When he rounded the bag, Jarrod thought he had a play and threw to third. His throw went wide of 3rd sacker Will Middlebrooks, who dove for the ball and in the process got tangled-up with Craig. The ball went to left field and Craig was accidentally tripped by Middlebrooks as he headed for home.

Home plate Umpire Jim Joyce ruled Craig out, but after much confusion reversed his call and Craig was declared safe on the seldom used obstruction call. The rule in the books could not measure intent, so whether tripping was real or accidental had no relevancy. This was the first time in World Series history that a game ended on obstruction.

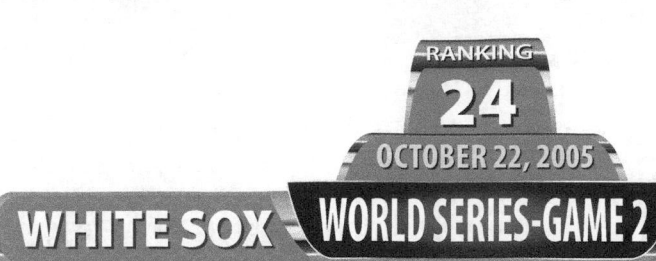

WHITE SOX — WORLD SERIES-GAME 2 — ASTROS

INNINGS

7   9   6

ACCIDENTAL HOMERUN

Outfielder Scott Podsednik, a left-hander known for stealing bases, hit a 2-1 fastball into the right field stands off Brad Lidge to win game two. Podsednik hadn't hit a homerun during the regular season, and in the ALDS had only 1-hit.

Leading the White Sox was colorful Manager "Ozzie" Guillen, who received a standing ovation from the home crowd in 2004 when he became skipper mid-season. Guillen had been a star shortstop for 16 seasons, playing for the Sox from 1985-1997. The "South Siders," who were never as popular as the Cubs, would sweep the Astros for their first championship since 1917.

BASEBALL TRIVIA

• *Podsednik's walk-off homerun in the bottom of the 9th was only the 14th in World Series history.*

YANKEES — ALDS-GAME 3 — ORIOLES

3 | INNINGS **12** | **2**

"A-ROD" SPECTATOR

Baltimore had a 2–1 lead going into the ninth inning, when Yankees Raul Ibañez hit his first of two home runs in the bottom of the 9th to tie the score.

Ibañez later crushed the first pitch of the 12th inning into the second deck of Yankee Stadium to win the game, allowing the Yankees to take a series lead in walk-off fashion. Yankees skipper Joe Girardi was lucky he made the gutsy decision to send Ibañez to pinch hit for the slumping Alex "A-Rod" Rodriguez in the 9th.

RAUL **IBANEZ**
NEW YORK YANKEES®　OF

BASEBALL TRIVIA

• *Ibañez, at age 40, is the oldest player to hit a homerun in the post season.*

• *He is also the only player to hit two home runs in a game in which he didn't start.*

• *Alex Rodriguez has a .295 career batting average, 3,115 hits and 696 home runs.*

• *Rodriguez signed a 10-year contract for $275 million, the most in history at the time. (An accusation of steroid use will probably prevent HOF status.)*

RANKING
26
SEPTEMBER 23, 1908
GIANTS
NL PENNANT RACE
CUBS
INNINGS
9

MERKLE'S BONER

MERKLE, N. Y. NAT'L

The most controversial moment in the history of the game led to a riot at the Polo Grounds, home of the New York Giants. Fans poured onto the field, thinking the Giants had defeated the Cubs. It turned out Giants rookie Fred Merkle had singled, but failed to touch second base after the apparent winning run scored. Merkle's failure to advance to second base on what should have been a game-winning hit led instead to a force-out at second and a tied game. This play became known as Merkle's Boner.

In a make-up game at the end of the season, the Cubs would win the game, deciding the NL pennant. Enraged Giants owner John T. Bush gave each team member a medal that read "The Real Champions 1908."

BASEBALL TRIVIA

Merkle was 19 years old when he played in this game, and was the youngest player in the National League at that time.

TWINS **WORLD SERIES-GAME 7** **BRAVES**

| 1 | INNINGS 10 | 0 |

I'M NOT LEAVING

The Series-deciding seventh game was a scoreless tie (0–0) through the regular nine innings, and went into extra innings. The pitching matchup was a repeat of game four, with Twins HOF Jack Morris vs. Braves HOF John Smoltz. Smoltz went 7.1 innings scoreless, and Morris went the distance.

JACK MORRIS P

Several times during the game Twins Manager Tom Kelly, known for as "Captain Hook," tried to remove Morris but he refused to go. A Twins sportswriter quipped at the time: "(Morris) could have outlasted Methuselah."

In the bottom of the 10th, injured Gene Larkin, the next to last position player on the bench, hit the World Series winning single.

Morris was named the Series MVP.

BASEBALL TRIVIA

• *During his career, Morris had 175 complete games among his 254 wins.*

GIANTS WIN THE PENNANT TWICE

The Cards led 3-2 entering the 8th inning, when relief pitcher Pat Neshek served-up a homerun to pinch-hitter Michael Morse to tie the game.

With 2 outs in the bottom of the 9th, Travis Ishikawa's 3-run shot off Michael Wacha sent the Giants to the World Series.

This hadn't happened since the Giants Bobby Thomson hit a walk-off homerun to send his team to the World Series in 1951. Thomson's shot was memorialized by the call: "The Giants win the pennant! The Giants win the pennant!"

BASEBALL TRIVIA

• *Travis Ishikawa started the season with the Pittsburgh Pirates as their starting first baseman, thn was traded to the Giants where he became the starting leftfielder*

• *Ishikawa's home run was the first ever to end an NLCS and the fourth to end any NLCS.*

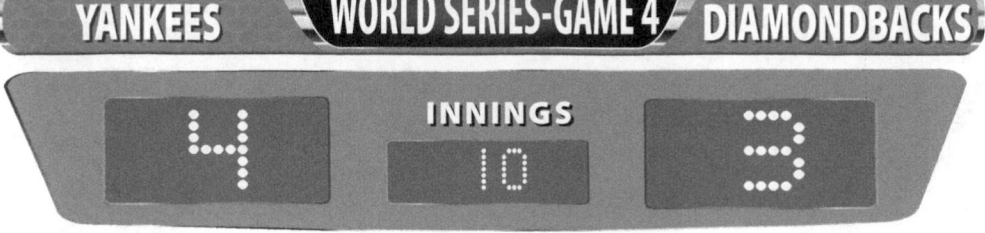

"MR. NOVEMBER"

The Diamondbacks led 3-1 heading to the bottom of the 8th. 'Backs Manager Bob Brenly elected to bring in closer Byung-hyun Kim, the first Korean born player to pitch in a Series, in relief of Curt Schilling.

Derek Jeter • SS
NEW YORK YANKEES

With 2-outs, Yankees first baseman Tino Martinez hit a 2-run blast into the right field bleachers, resulting in a tie game.

In the 10th, also with 2 outs, Kim threw a slider on the outside part of the plate, and Yankees Captain Derek Jeter hit an opposite field homerun for the victory. Jeter's heroics came just as the clock struck midnight and the Series went into November for the first time. This earned Jeter the nickname "Mr. November."

BASEBALL TRIVIA

• *After the first pitch to Jeter, a message was posted on the center-field scoreboard that read, "Attention fans: Welcome to November Baseball."*

METS WORLD SERIES-GAME 4 ORIOLES

INNINGS

2   10   1

"AMAZIN' METS" UPSET BIRDS

RON SWOBODA
Outfield

METS

Mets Pitcher "Tom Terrific" Seaver shut the Orioles out through eight innings. Donn Clendenon provided the lead with a homer in the second off Mike Cuellar, who allowed just that run over seven solid innings.

Ron Swoboda, not known for his fielding, made a spectacular catch in the right field of a ball hit by Brooks Robinson in the 9th to hold the Orioles rally to one.

In the bottom of the tenth, Jerry Grote led off with a double to left, and Al Weis was walked. Mets manager Gil Hodges sent J. C. Martin up to hit for Seaver. Martin laid down a sacrifice bunt, but Orioles reliever Pete Richert hit Martin in the wrist with his throw to first, and the ball went down the right field line. Rod Gaspar, running for Grote, came around to score the winning run in the biggest upset in World Series history.

BASEBALL TRIVIA

• *The nickname Amazin' Mets was coined by Casey Stengel.*

MARLINS — WORLD SERIES-GAME 7 — INDIANS

INNINGS

3 — 11 — 2

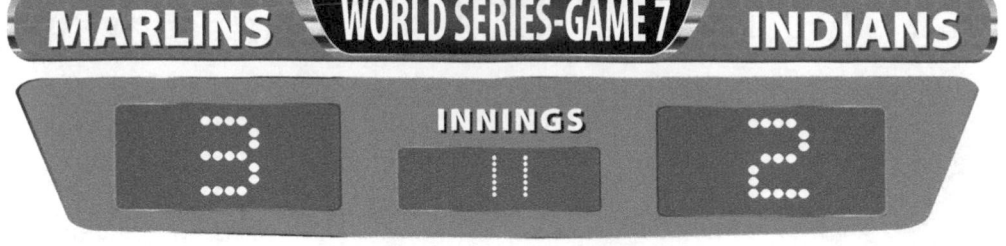

JOSÉ "CHOKER" MESA

Indians Manager Mike Hargrove decided to start rookie Jaret Wright on 3 days rest instead of the veteran Charles Nagy. He was rewarded when Wright pitched 6 innings of a one-hit shutout as the Indians led 2–0.

In the 7th, he gave-up a lead-off homerun to Bobby Bonilla, cutting the lead to 2-1.

Indians closer José Mesa came on in the 9th inning. With runners on 1st and 3rd and one out, Craig Counsell fought off a low, inside fastball from Mesa, lining it into deep right field. Manny Ramírez got the out, but Moisés Alou scored from third.

In the bottom of the 11th, relief pitcher Charles Nagy served-up a 2-out, bases loaded single to Edgar Rentería for the game winner.

BASEBALL TRIVIA

• *Teammate Omar Vazquel called Mesa a "choker" in his autobiography, because he blew the save in this game, allowing the Marlins to tie the game.*

DODGERS — WORLD SERIES-GAME 3 — RED SOX

INNINGS
3   18   2

MARATHON GAME

Pitching dominated early with Dodgers Walker Buehler going 7 scoreless innings, while his counterpart Rick Porcello went 4-2/3, only blemished by Joe Pederson's 2nd inning home run. Dodgers All-Star closer Kenley Jansen allowed a 2-run homer to Jackie Bradley Jr. with 2 outs in the top of the 8th, which tied the contest.

In the 13th inning each team scored a run — Red Sox's Eduardo Nunez singled in Brock Holt and in the last half of the inning an infield hit by Dodgers Yasiel Puig and a throwing error by Ian Kinsler allowed Max Muncy, who had walked, to score and tie the game.

The rest of the night belonged to Muncy, who had been called up on April 17 from Oklahoma City. In the 15th, he appeared to hit a walk-off homerun to right field, but the ball barely curved foul. Then, in the 18th Muncy went distance, making a loser of Nathan Eovaldi, who was starting his 7th inning of work.

BASEBALL TRIVIA

• *This "marathon" game was the longest in World Series history in both time, seven hours and 20 minutes, and innings at 18.*

DODGERS	NL WEST	PADRES
11	INNINGS 10	10

"4 + 1"

For the first time since 1964, the Dodgers hit four consecutive home runs in the bottom of the 9th, after trailing 9-5. The game, played at Dodgers Stadium before a capacity crowd of 55,831, was a battle for first place in the NL West. The 4 home runs were hit off two Padres relievers and came off the bats of Jeff Kent, J.D. Drew, Russell Martin and Marlon Anderson, who had a career day with 5 hits.

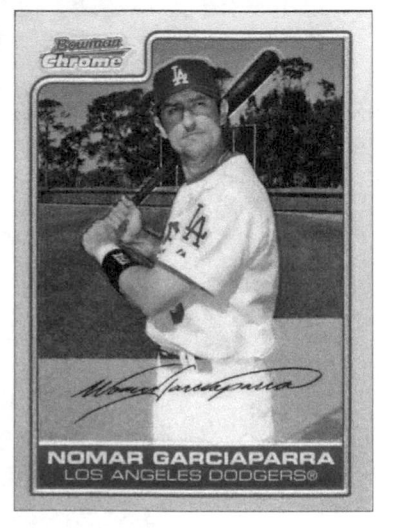

NOMAR GARCIAPARRA
LOS ANGELES DODGERS®

The Padres didn't quit there. They got the lead at the top of the 10th on a double by Brian Giles and a 2-out single by Josh Bard off Aaron Seles, who would later become the winning pitcher.

In the bottom of the 10th, Kenny Lofton walked and Nomar Garciaparra hit his 18th home run for the walk-off win.

BASEBALL TRIVIA

• *Garciaparra had missed several games due to a strained left quad and had to sweet talk Manager Grady Little to place his name in the lineup for this game.*

ROCKIES — NL 1-GAME PLAYOFF — PADRES

INNINGS

9 | 9 | 8

ROCKIES BACK FROM THE DEAD

TREVOR HOFFMAN
Padres™

In early September the Rockies won home field advantage on a coin toss if there was to be a playoff. The Rockies were always a better team at home. The Rockies were also a hot club, winning 21 of their last 22 regular season games.

In the top of the 9th, the Padres took the lead with 2 runs on a blast by Scott Hairston off Jorge Julio.

Heading to the bottom of the 9th, with the Padres down 8-6, they found themselves facing Trevor Hoffman, then the all-time save leader at 601.

The Padres went on to score 3 runs on key hits — doubles by Kaz Matsui and Troy Tulowitski, and a triple from Matt Holiday. Holiday went on to score the game winner on Jamey Carroll's sacrifice fly to right field. Sportswriters on the scene thought Holiday was out at the plate. On a bang-bang play Padres catcher Mike Barrett had the plate blocked but the throw bounced away. The home plate umpire ruled Holiday safe, even though replays showed he never touched home.

TIGERS   WORLD SERIES-GAME 6   CUBS

| 4 | INNINGS 9 | 3 |

STAR SITS TEAM WINS

Heading into the Series, the Tigers appeared destined to lose. They hadn't won a championship, and the Cubs had won 21 straight games — regular season record.

Tommy Bridges

Their star first baseman, Hank Greenberg, was out with a broken wrist suffered in game two. During the regular season, Greenberg drove in 170 runs and hit 36 homeruns. In the Series, his replacements had one hit in 36 at-bats.

In the top of the 9th the Tigers scored the winning run as "Goose" Goslin singled home HOF Player/Manager catcher Mickey Cochrane.

The star of the game was pitcher Tommy Bridges, who went the distance for the Tigers' first championship. Cochrane said Bridges was "a hundred and fifty pounds of courage. If there ever is a payoff on courage, this little 150-pound pitcher is the greatest World Series hero."

BASEBALL TRIVIA

• *Hank Greenberg, nicknamed "Hammerin' Hank," was the first Jewish baseball superstar.*

DODGERS — WORLD SERIES·GAME 4 — YANKEES

INNINGS

3 · 9 · 2

"THE COOKIE GAME"

HARRY LAVAGETTO
Third Base, Brooklyn, N.L.

The Yankees right hander Bill Bevens was one out away from completing the first no-hitter in World Series history. The Yankees, playing at Ebbets Field, led 2-0. In the 5th, the Dodgers would get one run back without a hit; two walks and a Pee Wee Reese fielder's choice. In the bottom of the 9th, Bevens lost both his no-hitter and the game. With one out, right fielder Carl "The Reading Rifle" Furillo walked. After 3rd baseman "Spider" Jorgensen fouled-out for the second out, Furillo was pinch-run by Al Gionfriddo, who promptly stole second.

Yankees skipper Bucky Harris elected to walk Pete Reiser with first base open, holding just a 1-run lead. "Cookie" Lavagetto pinch-hit for Eddie "The Brat" Stanky, and launched a line drive to right that hit the wall, and bounced off "Old Reliable" Tommy Heinrich's shoulder. Gionfriddo and Reiser had scored for the victory by the time he got the ball.

BASEBALL TRIVIA

• *This was the first integrated World Series. Jackie Robinson had joined the Dodgers April 15 as their first baseman.*

• *"Cookie" and Bevens would not appear in another Major League game.*

DODGERS   WORLD SERIES-GAME 7   YANKEES

| 2 | INNINGS
9 | 0 |

SANDY AMOROS AN UNLIKELY HERO

Johnny Podres won the Series MVP for this game, the first time the award was given, Sandy Amoros, the defensive replacement left fielder who entered the game in the 6th, was all anyone could talk about.

SANDY AMOROS outfield BROOKLYN DODGERS

In the 6th the first two batters, Billy "The Kid" Martin and Gil McDougald, were on first and second, as left-handed Yogi Berra came to bat. Berra hit a fly ball towards the left field line, when the Dodgers outfield had just shifted to the right. Out of nowhere came the speedy 5'7" Cuban born Amoros, who robbed Berra of a certain double. Amoros skidded to avoid the left field fence at the 301' mark, turned and threw the ball to the cutoff man, shortstop Pee Wee Reese who threw to Gil Hodges, doubling Gil McDougald. This gave the Dodgers their only championship while playing in Brooklyn.

BASEBALL TRIVIA

• *The Yankees defeated the Dodgers in World Series in 1947, 1949, 1953. This was the first World Series loss for the Yankees since 1942.*

• *The Dodgers moved to Los Angeles in 1957.*

RED SOX WORLD SERIES-GAME 8 GIANTS

3 INNINGS 2
10

THE $30,000 MUFF

SNODGRASS-NEWYORK-NAT.

Game 8 began in controversy over where it would be played. Eventually Boston's Fenway Park got the nod, but the crowd was understandably small, and the Red Sox's most loyal fans, the "Royal Rooters," were prevented from sitting in their regular seats.

At the top of the 10th, the game was tied. The Giants broke the tie on a "Red" Murray double, following a single by Fred Merkle. In the bottom of the 10th, pinch-hitter Clyde Engle opened by hitting a routine fly ball to Giants centerfielder Fred Snodgrass, and he dropped it resulting in a two-base error. Although Snodgrass would make a spectacular running catch on a shot by Harry Hooper, a single by Tris Speaker retied the contest, and a sacrifice fly by Larry Gardner won the game.

The Snodgrass error became known as the $30,000 Muff because it cost the Giants the $30,000 World Series championship bonus. This error would haunt Snodgrass to his grave — it was even mentioned in his obituary. Giants Manager John McGraw, when asked what he did to Snodgrass, remarked: "...I will tell you exactly what I did: I raised his salary $1,000."

THE RYAN EXPRESS RUNS OUT OF GAS

The Astros jumped to an early lead in the first on a run-scoring double by José Cruz. Philadelphia bounced back to take the lead on a two-run single by Bob Boone in the second.

The Phillies trailed 5–2, entering the 8th. The great HOF Nolan Ryan was on the mound. The Phillies, however, rallied with 5 runs, chasing Ryan.

The Astros promptly came back to tie the game in the bottom of the eighth. Neither team scored in the 9th.

At the top of the 10th, the Phillies put the game away on doubles by Del Unser and Greg Maddox.

This was their first pennant win since 1950.

BASEBALL TRIVIA

• *Nolan Ryan is the all-time strikeout leader at 5,714, his fastest fast ball on record is 108.5mph, he had 324 wins, and pitched the most no-hitters — seven.*

• *The biggest at-bat was a bases loaded walk by 39-year-old Pete Rose.*

DODGERS — NLW PENNANT DECIDER — GIANTS

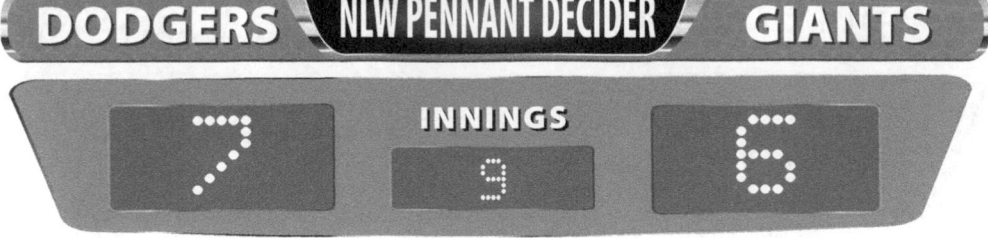

	INNINGS	
7	9	6

"IT AIN'T OVER 'TIL IT'S OVER"

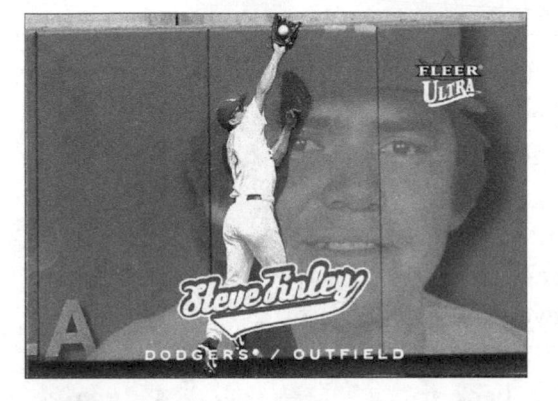

This was a game for the ages, featuring the most heated rivalry in the National League. Their feud dates to the late 19th century, and even continued when both clubs moved from NYC to the West Coast in 1957.

The Dodgers trailed 3-0 heading to the bottom of the 9th and with a win they would clinch the NL West Pennant. The Giants played a sloppy 9th, logging 3 walks and an error.

With one out and the bases loaded, the Dodgers were trailing 3-2 when Steve Finley hit a grand slam home run off lefty Wayne Franklin. Dodgers reliever Eric Gagne said if the win, "We do it the Hollywood way."

BASEBALL TRIVIA

• *The Diamondbacks had traded 39-year old Finley and Brent Way to the Dodgers in July for Kayie Hill, Reggie Abercombie and Bill Murphy.*

SO MUCH FOR PITCH COUNT ANALYTICS

The Nationals, with the best record in the Majors at 98 wins, and playing in Washington D.C. for the NL pennant last won in 1933 were 1-strike away from going to the NLCS. The Nationals led 6-0 after 3-innings and 7-5 entering the 9th.

STEPHEN STRASBURG
PITCHER

Nationals closer Drew Storen gave up 4 runs in the top of the inning, silencing the home crowd on 2-run singles from both Daniel Descalso and Pete Kozma. St. Louis had clinched a trip to the NLCS for the second straight year.

Nationals GM Mike Rizzo was heavily criticized for shutting down their ace, Stephen Strasburg, for the entire series on September 8. He was on a strict pitch count as a result of undergoing Tommy John surgery (ulnar collateral ligament reconstruction). Before the shutdown, Strasburg went 15–6 with an ERA of 3.16. Strasburg was the #1 pick in the 2009 draft and according to ESPN was "the most hyped pick in draft history."

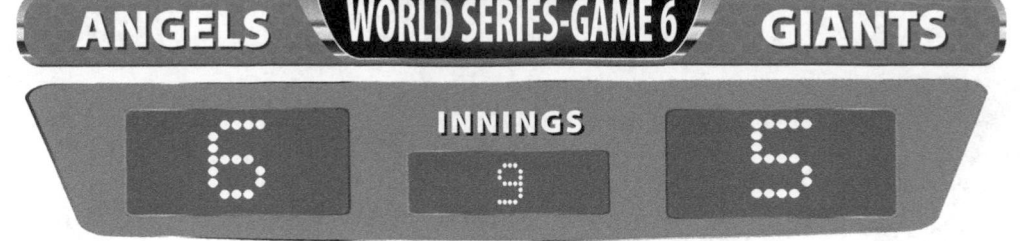

OCTOBER 26, 2002

ANGELS WORLD SERIES-GAME 6 **GIANTS**

INNINGS

6   9   5

"RALLY MONKEY"

The Giants led 5-0 heading to the bottom of the 7th. Manager Dusty Baker made a surprising pitching change, removing starter Russ Ortiz in favor of set-up man Felix Rodriguez. In the midst of the changeover the "Rally Monkey" appeared on the JumboTron, sending the 45,037 home fans in to a frenzy.

From that point on it was all Angels. Scott Spiezio and Darin Erstad went deep, closing the gap to 5–4.

Against Giants closer Robb Nen in the 8th a 2-run double to left center by Troy Glaus turned out to be the game winner.

BASEBALL TRIVIA

• *Overcoming the 5-0 deficit was the biggest in a World Series elimination game.*

• *The Angels went on to win the Series at home in game seven, breaking the supposed curse on Anaheim for building its stadium on an ancient Indian burial ground.*

"THE SLIDE"

Pirates starter Doug Drabek was pitching a masterpiece headed in to the bottom of the 9th, with the Pirates leading 2–0. He was replaced by Stan Belenda, who re-loaded the bases after allowing a scoring single by Braves pinch-hitter Francisco Carbrera.

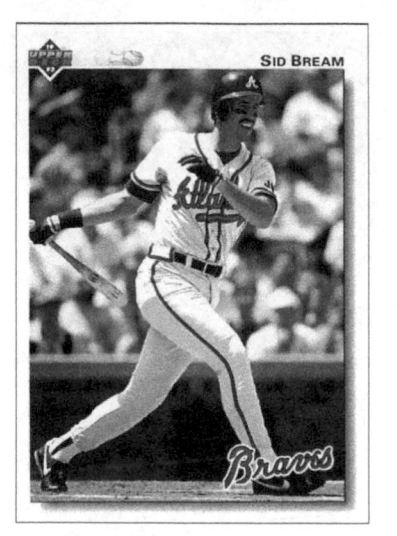

A single to left center scored Dave Justice from 3rd, as slow-footed Sid Bream attempted to score from second. The throw from nine-time Gold Glove left-fielder Barry Bonds arrived in time, but was wide and Bream scored the game winner.

BASEBALL TRIVIA

• *This was the last game where Barry Bonds would appear in a Pirates uniform. He went on to play 14 seasons with the San Francisco Giants. When he retired he had a .298 batting average, 2,935 hits and 762 homeruns — the most ever. Despite his stellar career, a steroids use scandal might keep him from the Hall of Fame.*

SINGING COWBOY DENIED

DONNIE MOORE

Angels pitching ace, Mike Witt, entered the 9th inning with a 4-run lead, looking for his second complete game of the series. The champagne was on ice in the dugout so the players could toast their beloved owner, Gene Autry "The Singing Cowboy."

Witt served up a 2-run homerun to Don Baylor, and Angels closer Donnie Moore was brought in to face Dave Henderson. Earlier, Henderson the Angels centerfielder had jumped high to catch a long fly off the bat of Bobby Grinch but deflected the ball in to the stands for a homerun. This time Henderson atoned for his misplay by blasting a 2-run shot on a 2-srike count putting the Angels up by 1-run.

The Angels came back to tie the game on a single by Rod Wilfong but left the bases loaded with 1-out sending the game in to extra innings. In the 11th Henderson did it again, hitting a sacrifice fly, scoring the winning run.

BASEBALL TRIVIA

• *Gene Autry's number 26 was retired by the California Angels in 1982.*

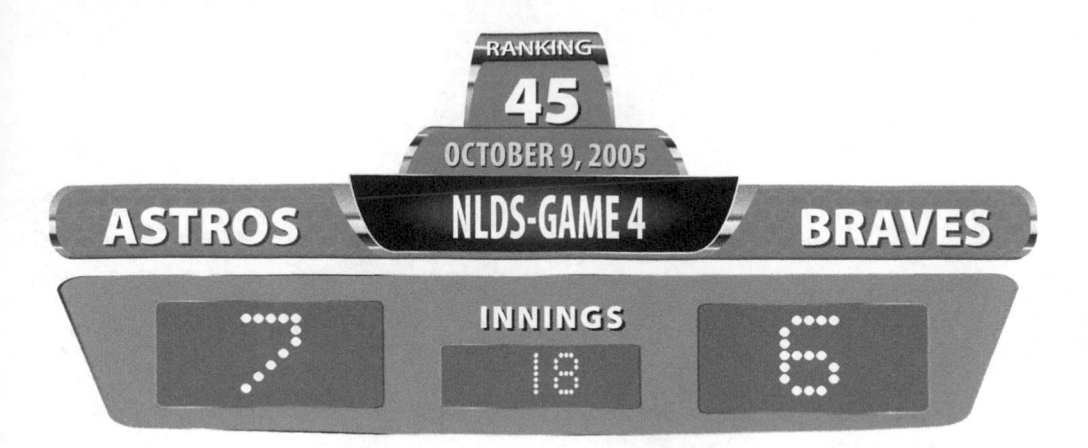

ASTROS   BRAVES

INNINGS

7   18   6

18 INNINGS DECIDES

It took 18-innings, but the home run ball was the difference. First the Braves Adam La Roche hit a grand slam home run in the 3rd, propelling the Braves to a 6–1 lead as they entered the bottom of the 8th.

CHRIS BURKE
SECOND BASE

Kyle Farnsworth, in relief, was victimized by a grand slam homer off the bat of Lance Berkman, and a tying shot in the 9th by Brad Ausmus with 2-outs.

In the 18th Chris Burke went deep off rookie Joey Devine for the win.

BASEBALL TRIVIA

• *Fan Shaun Dean, sitting in Section 102, Row 2, Seat 15, caught both Berkman's and Burke's home runs. He donated the balls to the HOF.*

"THE DOUBLE"

The Seattle Mariners roared back from a 2–0 game deficit and a 4–2 Yankees lead in the 8th inning of deciding game five.

In the 8th a Ken Griffey Jr. home run followed by a bases-loaded walk tied the game.

The Yankees gained the lead in the top of the 11th when Randy Velarde singled off Randy "The Big Unit" Johnson, who was making a rare relief appearance.

The Mariners came back once again, this time on a 2-run double by DH Edgar Martinez off Jack McDowell to win the Series.

This hit will forever be remembered as "The Double."

BASEBALL TRIVIA

• *Martinez won the AL batting title, hitting .356.*

• *Both Martinez and Griffey Jr. made it to the Hall of Fame.*

• *This win kept the Mariners franchise in Seattle, because it motivated voters to approve a bond issue for the new Safeco Stadium.*

YANKEES — WORLD SERIES-GAME 4 — BRAVES

INNINGS

8   10   6

BAT TWIRLING WORKS

Jim Leyritz, known for twirling his bat at the hip — a trick he learned from teammate Mickey Rivers, had the biggest hit of his career. It was a 3-run home run in the top of the 8th off closer Mark Wohlers to tie the game. This was a surprise to everyone, because Leyritz didn't have great hitting ability and only remained on the ball club from 1990–1996 because star lefty Andy Pettitte insisted Leyritz be his exclusive catcher.

A bases loaded walk by batting champion Wade Boggs in the top of the 10th turned out to be the game winner.

BASEBALL TRIVIA

• *Wade Boggs was a five-time AL batting champion who had 1412 walks, 3,010 hits and a career batting average of .328.*

STOLEN HOME PLATE DOESN'T MATTER

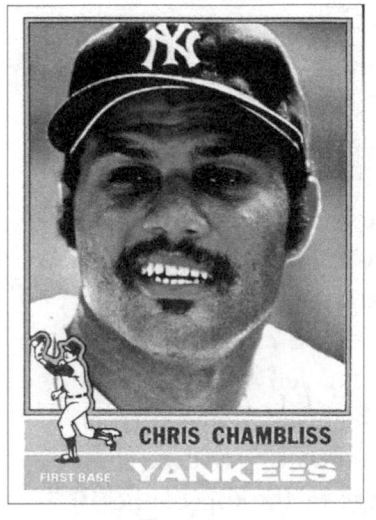

CHRIS CHAMBLISS
FIRST BASE YANKEES

The Yankees led 6–3 at the top of the 8th, when one of the game's great hitters, George Brett, unloaded a 3-run homer for the tie. Yankees on-and-off-again manager Billy "The Kid" Martin, five-times the Yankees skipper, had sent lefty Grant Jackson to face Brett — in a classic lefty vs. lefty matchup.

In the bottom of the 9th, Yankees first baseman Chris Chambliss hit the first pitch from Mark Littell over the right field wall for the series win. The home crowd stormed the field, and Chambliss, who was rounding second base, fled for his life and made it safely to the dugout without touching home plate. Later, Chambliss was escorted onto the field to touch home, but the plate had been stolen, so he touched the area where the plate had been. Umpires counted the run.

BASEBALL TRIVIA

• *The Yankees would defeat the Royals in three consecutive playoff series beginning with this win.*

RED SOX   **WORLD SERIES-GAME 2**   ROBINS

	INNINGS	
2	14	1

BABE RUTH STARS ON THE MOUND

The Robins scored in the top of the 1st on an inside-the-park home run by Hy Myers, and the Red Sox tied it in the bottom of the third, with Babe Ruth knocking in the run with a ground ball.

The game remained 1–1 until the bottom of the 14th, when a pinch-hit single by Del Gainer made Ruth the winner.*

BASEBALL TRIVIA

• *Ruth pitched 13 scoreless innings in this game.*

• *At the time, this game set a Word Series record for the longest game by innings.*

BABE RUTH
P.—Boston Red Sox
151

• *Ruth's impressive pitching statistics in 1916 were: 23 wins, 170 strikeouts, 1.75 era, 9-shutouts and 23 complete games.*

• *Babe Ruth was traded to the Yankees in 1919.*

* *Note: dead ball era.*

PHILLY A's — WORLD SERIES-GAME 4 — CUBS

	INNINGS	
10	9	8

"MACK ATTACK"

The Cubs scored 7 runs off starting pitcher Jack Quinn before Manager Connie Mack pulled him in the 6th inning, setting the stage for the "Mack Attack" in the bottom of the seventh.

After seven-and-a-half innings, the Cubs had an 8–0 lead. One out, two lost balls in the sun and 13 batters later, the Cubs found themselves losing 10–8.

The key play of the game was when Hack Wilson lost Mule Haas' fly ball in the sun, resulting in a bases-clearing, inside-the-park home run. Since Wilson didn't touch the ball, it was ruled an-inside-the park home run. (This was the second ball lost in the sun for Wilson in this game.)

BASEBALL TRIVIA

• "Hack," standing just 5'6", rivaled Babe Ruth as a power hitter. In 1930, he hit 56 home runs and 191 RBIs, a record that still stands.

• The A's owner/Manager Connie Mack wore a 3-piece suit and sat in the dugout for the first 50 years of the franchise, before retiring at age 87.

GAME WINNING GRAND SLAM SINGLE

The Mets' season appeared over after Keith Lockhart tripled home a run in the top of the 15th off Octavio Dotel to put the Braves ahead 3–2. However, pitcher Kevin McGlinchy could not hold the lead.

An injured Robin Ventura, who played it out on one leg all day, hit a grand slam single in the bottom of the 15th for the win. Although Ventura had seen the ball clear the wall, and was waving Pratt around the bases, Pratt tackled Ventura between first and second base, and most of the Mets team ran out on the field and mobbed Ventura in a wild scene.

BASEBALL TRIVIA

• *At the time, the game was the longest in terms of elapsed time in postseason history, clocking in at 5 hours, 46 minutes.*

• *This Mets victory marked just the second time in baseball history that a team had come back from a three games to none deficit in a best-of-seven series to make it to a Game 6.*

51

KENDRICK REVENGE

Howie Kendrick   **2ND BASE**

In deciding game 5 in Los Angeles, the Dodgers led 3-0 after 5 innings. Back-to-back home runs in the eighth by Anthony Rendon and Juan Soto off Clayton Kershaw, who was making a rare relief appearance, tied the game.

With a scoreless ninth inning, the game went to extra innings. In the top of the 10th, former Dodger Howie Kendrick silenced the home crowd with a grand slam off of Joe Kelly in the top of the tenth inning, giving the Nationals a 7–3 lead.

Sean Doolittle sent down the Dodgers in order in the bottom of the 10th, getting Justin Turner to fly out to Michael Taylor for the third out. The Dodgers called for a video review, but the call was upheld and it ended the series.

BASEBALL TRIVIA

- *This was the first NLDS Game 5 to go into extra innings since 2011.*
- *Clayton Kershaw won the NL Cy Young award three times and NL MVP once.*
- *This was the third straight year and fourth time in the last five years the Dodgers were eliminated from the postseason at home.*

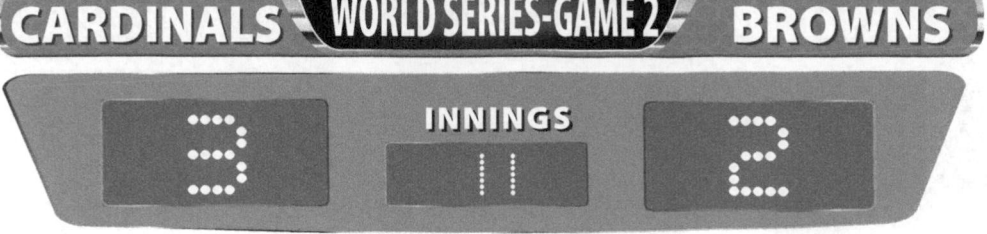

OCTOBER 5, 1944

CARDINALS — WORLD SERIES-GAME 2 — BROWNS

INNINGS

3 | 11 | 2

"TROLLEY SERIES"

In the 8th inning the Cardinals Manager Billy Southworth went to rookie relief pitcher Bix Donnelly and he delivered; no runs, two hits and 7-strikeouts.

In the bottom of the 11th, the Browns Bob Muncrief was on the mound when backup catcher Ken O'Dea's pinch-hit single brought in the winning run. The heavily favored Cards would go on to win the Series.

Ken O'Dea   Catcher
1942-1946   St. Louis Cardinals

BASEBALL TRIVIA

• *This Series was nicknamed "The Trolley Series" after the MGM movie Meet Me in St. Louis, starring Judy Garland, that opened the same year.*

• *Both rosters were filled with so-called 4F athletes, because regular players had been drafted to serve in World War II.*

• *1944 marked the only year the Browns would win the AL pennant.*

• *This was the last time in World Series history that both teams played in the same ballpark —Sportsman Park.*

CHAPMAN'S "SAD SMILE"

In the bottom of the sixth, Alex Bregman hit into a fielder's choice, scoring the fourth run for the Astros. In the top of the 9th inning, an Gio Urshela single was followed two batters later by a DJ LeMahieu home run that tied the game at 4. After George Springer extended the bottom of the ninth with a two-out walk, José Altuve hit a walk-off two-run home run off Aroldis Chapman to win the game and send the Astros to their second World Series in three years.

Jose Altuve, the Series MVP, then hit a high curve ball out of Minute Maid Park to end the Series. Yankees closer Aroldis Chapman was seen smiling and watching Altuve celebrate, knowing he should have thrown his money pitch, the 100mph+ heater.

BASEBALL TRIVIA

• *With this loss the 2010s became the first decade since the 1910s not to have the Yankees play in a World Series.*

TIGERS   CWS FINAL   **HURRICANES**

9   INNINGS 9   8

BROKEN WRIST NOT A FACTOR

The game came down to the last of the 9th. LSU needed one run to tie, and two to win. The unlikely hero turned out to be #9 hitter Warren Morris, a pre-med student on an academic scholarship.

Morris had missed 39 games during the year with a broken wrist, and a week before the game had trouble gripping the bat. Morris went deep off All-American Miami pitcher Robbie Morrison, and had his first home run of the season.

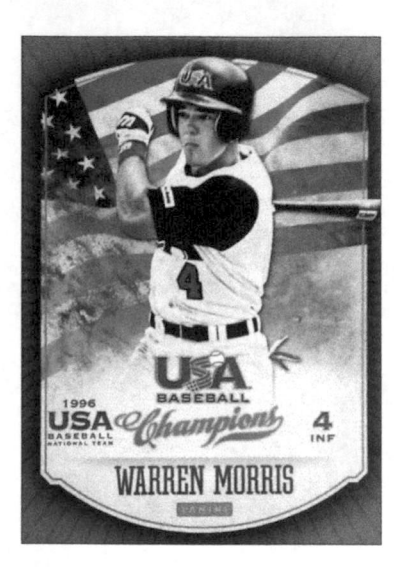

BASEBALL TRIVIA

• *This is the only game in CWS history where the championship was decided by a walk-off home run on the last pitch.*

• *LSU a perennial powerhouse won championships in 1991, 1993, 1996, 1997, 2000, and 2009.*

MOOSE IS LOSE

BOB MOOSE

After rain delayed the start of the game for 90 minutes, Pittsburgh took an early 2–0 lead in the second inning, and would hold onto their lead, staying ahead by one run, until the bottom of the 9th when Closer Dave Gusti gave up a home run to HOF catcher Johnny Bench to tie the game. Gusti was then was replaced by Bob Moose.

Tony Pérez singled and was replaced by pinch-runner George Foster. Denis Menke followed with a single, moving Foster to second base, then with the count 2-0 on César Geronimo, Giusti was replaced with Bob Moose. Geronimo's fly ball out advanced Foster to third base. Moose then uncorked a wild pitch to pinch-hitter Hal McRae, scoring Foster with the winning run.

BASEBALL TRIVIA

• *This was only the second time a postseason series ended on a wild pitch*

• *This was Pirates HOF right fielder Roberto Clemente's last on-field appearance. He was killed in a plane crash on December 31, 1972, while delivering supplies to earthquake victims in his native Nicaragua.*

DOUBLE NO-HITTER

Fred Toney dueled with Cubs pitcher Hippo Vaughn going nine hitless innings. In the top of the 10th, the Reds scored the only and winning run on a tapped ball in front of the plate by the speedy Jim Thorpe. Toney retired the Cubs in order in the bottom of the inning preserving the shutout, no-hitter and win.

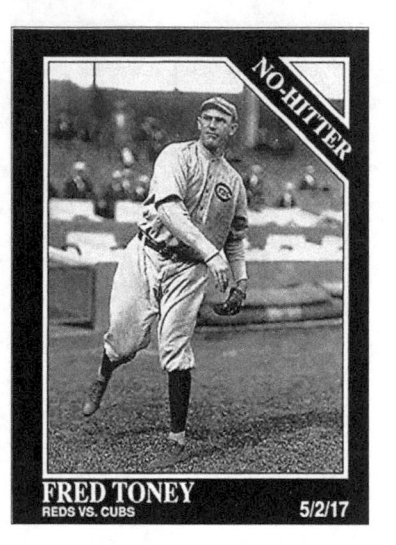

NO-HITTER

FRED TONEY
REDS VS. CUBS   5/2/17

BASEBALL TRIVIA

• *On July 1, 1917, Toney pitched two complete-game, three-hitters for victories in a doubleheader against the Pittsburgh Pirates, to set a record for fewest hits allowed in a double header by a Major League pitcher.*

• *Jim Thorpe who would also play professional football, and won the Olympic Decathlon Championship at the 1912 Stockholm games, where King Gustav V proclaimed him the World's Greatest Athlete.*

• *With changes to the scoring rules in recent years, this game is no longer considered as a no-hitter for Vaughn; but it is still the only occasion in Major League history in which a regulation nine innings was played without either team logging a hit. (The live ball era didn't begin until 1920.)*

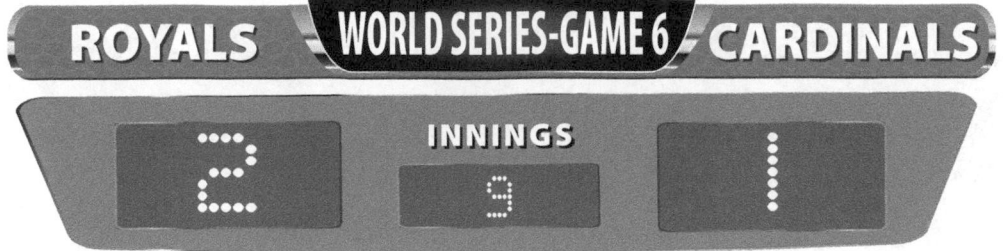

ROYALS · WORLD SERIES-GAME 6 · CARDINALS

INNINGS
2 | 9 | 1

"THE CALL"

In the bottom of the ninth, Whitey Herzog called on rookie reliever Todd Worrell to relieve setup man Ken Dayley, who had pitched the eighth. The first batter, pinch-hitter Jorge Orta, sent a chopping bouncer to the right of Jack Clark, who tossed to Worrell, who tagged the bag ahead of Orta. The probelm was, Clark's toss was behind Worrell and it allowed Orta to come between umpire Don Denkinger and his view of Worrell's glove. Denkinger called Orta safe. Replays indicated that Orta should have been called out, and an argument ensued on the field. Denkinger would not reverse the call and Orta remained at first.

With first base open and two runners in scoring position, Herzog chose to walk pinch-hitter Hal McRae to set up a potential double-play. John Wathan was sent to pinch-run for McRae. With the bases loaded and one out, pinch-hitter Dane Iorg blooped a single to right field. Pinch runner Onix Concepción scored the tying run with Jim Sundberg just behind sliding safely home for the win.

THE JEFFREY MAIER INCIDENT

Derek Jeter came to bat at the bottom of the 8th with his team behind by one run. Jeter hit an opposite field fly ball that headed towards the friendly right field wall, barely avoiding the outstretched hands of 11-year Yankees fan Jeffrey Maier.

Right field Umpire Jerry Garcia signaled a home run and then reaffirmed his decision after speaking with his crew.

Orioles Manager Davey Johnson protested, saying right fielder Tony Tarasco was interfered with. Johnson was ejected and the protest to Commissioner Bud Selig was denied.

In the bottom of the 11th switch-hitter Yankee centerfielder Bernie Williams, batting right handed, homered to scored off Randy Meyers for the victory.

BASEBALL TRIVIA

• *Bernie Williams later became a professional guitar player.*

OCTOBER 10, 1964

YANKEES — **WORLD SERIES-GAME 3** — **CARDINALS**

2   INNINGS   1
9

MANTLE SENDS HOWARD TO THE CLUBHOUSE

The Yankees scored a run in the second on Clete Boyer's RBI double with two on, but Simmons's RBI single tied the game in the 5th. Jim Bouton stranded the go-ahead run four times and held the top five hitters in the Cardinal lineup to a 2 for 21 day.

In the bottom of the 9th, Mickey Mantle was the leadoff hitter, with the game tied at one. He told on-deck hitter Elston Howard to go back to the clubhouse because he was going to hit a home run. Mantle swung at the first pitch from Barney Schultz, a knuckleball, and hit it into the right field stands to win the game.

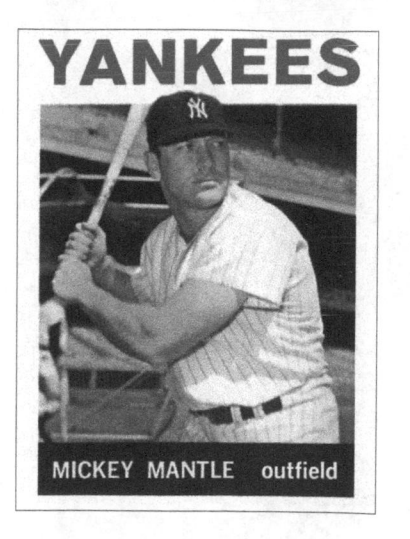

YANKEES

MICKEY MANTLE   outfield

BASEBALL TRIVIA

• *Mantle's home run (his 16th Series home run) broke Babe Ruth's record for most home runs hit in World Series play.*

• *Jim Bouton is the author of* Ball Four, *the first tell-all book in sports. Mantle felt the book tarnished his image and didn't speak to Bouton until shortly before his death in 1995.*

• *Elston Howard was the first African-American to play for the Yankees and he won the league MVP in 1963.*

OAKLAND A's — WORLD SERIES-GAME 2 — REDS

	INNINGS	
2	9	1

JOE RUDI CIRCUS CATCH

JOE RUDI

The Game 2 hero was A's left fielder Joe Rudi, who smacked a home run and added a game-saving catch up against the wall in the ninth inning on a ball hit by Denis Menke.

Catfish Hunter pitched eight strong innings, and also added an RBI single in the second off Ross Grimsley.

Cincinnati had leadoff baserunners in five innings but only scored a run in the ninth.

In the ninth, Tony Pérez led off with a base hit before Rudi's catch of Menke's drive for the first out. Rollie Fingers relieved Hunter and pinch hitter Julián Javier to popped out to Hegan to end the game.

BASEBALL TRIVIA

• *Jackie Robinson, the first black major league player of the modern era, made his final public appearance in Cincinnati before Game 2 (he died nine days later).*

• *Charles O. Finley set up a competition and offered $500 to any player that grew a mustache by Father's Day. The whole team participated and the A's became known as The Mustache Gang.*

THE HOMER IN THE GLOAMIN'

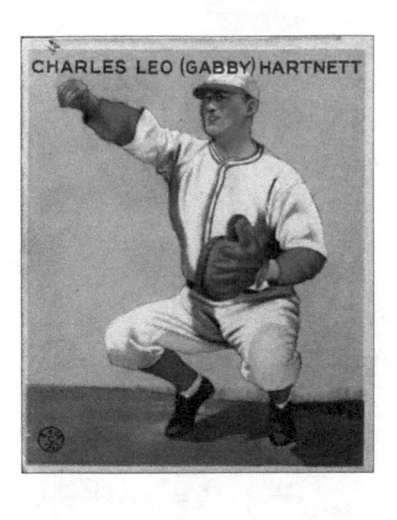

CHARLES LEO (GABBY) HARTNETT

Cubs Player/Manager Gabby Harnett, who was considered the best backstop prior to Johnny Bench, hit a 2-out walk-off home run to left center off Mace Brown with the game about to be called due to darkness. It is considered one of the most famous home runs in baseball folklore.

Harnett's blast was referred to as a Homer in the Glomin'. The expression was a play on a song popular at the time, "Roamin' in the Gloamin'" by Harry Lander.

BASEBALL TRIVIA

• *HOF Harnett broke the homerun record for catchers with 24 in 1925.*

• *Harnett led the league in errors, but was a superb defensive catcher. He was number-one in assists, caught stealing percentage, and shutouts.*

• *In 1934, Cubs president, Bill "Sport Shirt" Veeck, went to owner William Wrigley to add lights to Wrigley Field , but Wrigley thought lights were a fad. Wrigley Field finally got lights in 1988.*

RANKING
63
AUGUST 26, 2007
LLWS CHAMPIONSHIP
GEORGIA   TOKYO

2   INNINGS   1
8

LITTLE LEAGUE

In the 61st Little League World Series, the U.S. champion from Warner Robins, Georgia, defeated the international champion from Tokyo, Japan, 3–2 in extra innings (the game went 8 innings and regulation is 6).

In the 8th, leadoff batter Georgia shortstop Dalton Carriker, batting .769 hit a shot over the right field fence for the walk-off win.

Kendall Scott was the pitching star for Georgia, earning the save after throwing 5.2 innings of one-hit ball.

BASEBALL TRIVIA

• *The U.S. House of Representatives passed resolution 630 congratulating the winning team.*

• *This was the second straight year that a team from Georgia won the championship.*

• *Little League baseball dates to 1939, but the World Series didn't become a major sport until it was televised in 1984 by ABC Wide World of Sports.*

• *The championship final was the third elimination game in the tournament to end with a walk-off homer.*

GIANTS WORLD SERIES-GAME 3 RED SOX

INNINGS

2 9 1

WHO NEEDS A GLOVE?

DEVORE - NEW YORK - NAT.

Giants pitcher Rube Marquard pitched a complete game for the 2–1 victory, but it was not an easy one.

The Giants led 2–0 heading into the bottom of the 9th. With one out, Duffy Lewis reached first base on an infield single after Marquard couldn't locate first base.

Larry Gardner's double scored one, reducing the lead to 2–1. Later in the frame, with 2-outs, Olaf Henderson was on 3rd and Heinie Wagner, the potential winning run was on second. Nick Cady came up to bat and lined to right. Giants right fielder Josh Devore missed the fly ball with his glove, but managed to catch it with his bare left hand, ending the game.*

*This was a dead ball era game.

CARDINALS — WORLD SERIES-GAME 7 — RED SOX

4 — INNINGS 9 — 3

THE MAD DASH HOME

The Red Sox scored first with Dom DiMaggio's sacrifice fly after two leadoff singles off Murry Dickson. The Cardinals tied the game in the second.

By the 8th inning, the Cardinals were in the lead 3–1, when Dom DiMaggio tied the game with a two-run double but was pulled from the game due to a pulled a hamstring, and Leon Culberson took his position in center field.

"Harry the Hat" Walker lined to left center as Enos "Country" Slaughter on first rounded the bases. He was expected to stop at third base as Culberson fielded the ball and threw to the cutoff man

ENOS SLAUGHTER

Johnny Pesky. Cards third base Coach Mike Gonzalez flashed the sign for Slaughter to hold at third base but he ran through the sign, scoring what turned out to be the winning series run.

Pesky's delayed, weak, and rushed throw home allowed Slaughter to score just as Red Sox catcher Roy Partee caught it up the line from home plate.

PIRATES — WORLD SERIES-GAME 7 — SENATORS

INNINGS

9   9   7

"SLOGGIN' TO TRIUMPH"

Peckinpaugh
INFIELDER WASHINGTON AM.L

The Pirates hit Walter Johnson hard for 15 hits in a 9-7 comeback win in rainy, wet and muddy conditions.

In the 4th, Joe Harris hit a two-run double that made the score 6–3. Back-to-back doubles by Max Carey and Kiki Cuyler in the 5th cut the lead to 6–4, then in the 7th, Ray Moore reached first on an error before Carey's RBI double and Pie Traynor's RBI triple tied the game.

Senators Roger Peckinpaugh's home run in the 8th off Ray Kremer put the game at 7–6, but in the bottom half, back-to-back two-out doubles by Earl Smith and Carson Bigbee tied the game.

A walk and fielder's choice loaded the bases before Cuyler's two-run double, and the Pirates were in the lead 9–7. Red Oldham retired the Senators in order in the ninth to end the Series.

BASEBALL TRIVIA

• *The Pirates were the first team to come back from a 3–1 deficit in a seven-game Series.*

AMERICANS · AL PENNANT RACE · HIGHLANDERS

	INNINGS	
3	9	2

WILD PITCH DECIDES

For the first time in history, the Yankees (Highlanders) and Red Sox (Americans)would meet to decide the AL Pennant on the last day of the season. Played in the Bronx, NYC, at Hilltop Park, the Yankees would have to win at least one game of the doubleheader and tie the other. Boston was the defending champion and 200 of their fans traveled including the "Royal Rooters" supported by the Dockstader's Famous Minstrel Band. Behind HOF pitcher "Happy Jack" Chesbro the Yankees led 2–0 after 6-innings. The Red Sox however would tie the contest at 2–2 and win the game in the

top of the 9th on a wild pitch by Chesbro that cleared the glove of "Red" Kleinow.

BASEBALL TRIVIA

• *There was no World Series in1904 because the Giants refused to play an AL team.*

• *Chesbro had the greatest year in baseball pitching history: 41 wins, 51 games started, 48 complete games.*

TWO-DAY GAME

HAROLD BAINES OF

The game was halted in the top of the 18th at Comisky Park, and continued the following day. Harold Baines, former White Sox batting coach, was the walk-off hero, hitting a 1 out home run off Chuck Porter.

The Brewers led 3–1 after 8 innings, and were ahead again 6–3 heading to the bottom of the 21st. Brewers Ben Oglivie's 3-run homer was offset in the bottom of the 21st by a 2 run single off the bat of White Sox Tom Paciorek.

Former Mets HOF pitcher "Tom Terrific" Seaver, who was 40 at the time, went 1 inning in relief for the win.

BASEBALL TRIVIA

• *This was the first MLB game to go over 8 hours — by 6 minutes.*

• *This game went a total of 25 innings; the most in AL history.*

• *Harold Baines had a career 384 home runs and 2,836 hits. He finally made it to the HOF in 2019.*

On May 9, the teams met again and Seaver would walk-off with the win, throwing 8-1/3 innings for 2-wins in back-to-back games, which is a rarity.

ROYALS OVER THE HUMP

The Royals had lost to the Yankees in the post season for three consecutive years-1976, 1977 and 1978 but in 1980 they would finally get even, sweeping the Yankees in three straight games.

The hero was left-handed hitting HOF 3rd baseman George Brett. In the top of the 7th with his team trailing 2-1, two Royals on base and closer "Goose" Gossage having replaced Tommy John-(best known for the medical procedure Tommy John Surgery), Brett tomahawked a 97mph fast ball into the 3rd deck at Yankee Stadium. With the bases loaded in the 8th and no outs, the Yankees failed to score as All-Star sidearm, right-handed reliever Dan Quisenberry shut the door.

BASEBALL TRIVIA

• *George Brett played for the Royals for 21 years.*

• *Brett is one of the few to belong to the 3,000 hit club, while batting over .305 with 317 home runs.*

• *1980 was a career year for Brett, who flirted with .400 before finishing .390.*

• *In 1983 Brett would homer off Gossage in the famous Pine Tar bat incident.*

THE "WIZARD" GOES SOUTHPAW

Ozzie "The Wizard" Smith, arguably the greatest defensive shortstop of all time, won this game with his bat. The switch-hitting Smith homered on a ball barely cleared the right field wall off Tom Niedenfeuer with 1-out in the bottom of the 9th for the walk-off victory.

BASEBALL TRIVIA

• *Ozzie Smith won 13 consecutive Gold Glove Awards from 1980-1992, he also had the most career assists with 8,375, and the most double plays — 1,590.*

• *Smith's home run was voted the greatest moment in the history of Busch Stadium. Smith had never homered from the left side. He had just 28 home runs in his 18-year Major League career.*

• *Smith went in to the HOF in 2002, his first year of eligibility.*

• *Smith was traded from the Padres on December 10, 1981 for fellow shortstop Gary Templeton in a 6-player deal-both Smith and Templeton were having difficulties with their current managers.*

OROSCO TO THE RESCUE

The Astros jumped to a 3–0 in the first and southpaw Bob Knepper dominant throughout carried a shutout in to the 9th inning.

In the top of the 9th double by Keith Hernandez scored the 2nd run of the frame, chasing Knepper in favor of reliever Dave Smith.

A sacrifice fly by Ray Knight tied the score, sending the game in to extra innings. In the top of the 14th the Mets scored one on a Wally Backman hit, only to have the Astros Bill Hatcher hit a home run off the left field foul pole for a tie.

JESSE OROSCO

The Mets would go up by 3 runs in the 16th, just enough to offset the Astros, who scored twice. Lefty reliever Jesse Orosco finally ended the contest, striking out Kevin Bass with 2 runners on base.

BASEBALL TRIVIA

• *Orosco won three games in relief in the series without a loss, a post season record.*

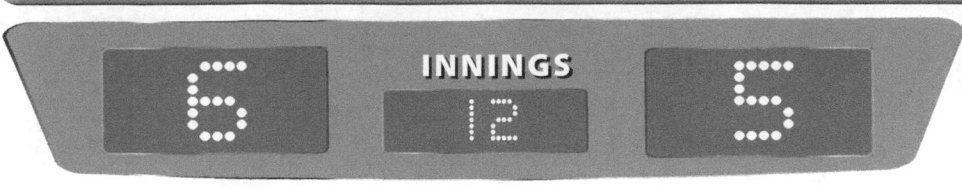

TWINS | AL CENTRAL TIE-BREAKER | TIGERS

6 INNINGS **12** **5**

GAME 163

In the 163rd game of the season — the last to be played at Hubert Humphrey Metrodome — the Twins outlasted the Tigers at home to win the AL Central.

Both teams finished the regular season with 86–76 records, but the Twins, by winning the regular series 11–7, were awarded this home field advantage.

In the top of the 12th, the Tigers appeared to take the lead, but home plate Umpire Randy Marsh ruled a bases loaded pitch did not hit batter Brandon Inge.

ALEXI CASILLA

In the home half of the 12th, with closer Fernando Rodney on the hill, a single by Alexi Casilla scored the speedy Carlos Gomez with the winning run.

INNINGS

5   12   4

"CHARLIE HUSTLE"

This 41st All-Star game was played at the brand-new Riverfront Stadium, home of the Reds. The NL was down 3 runs in their home half of the 9th but rallied behind a Dick Deitz homer, Willie McCovey single, and Roberto Clemente sacrifice fly to send the game into extra innings.

The NL's final run, scored in the bottom of the 12th by Pete Rose, the ball was relayed to the AL catcher, Ray Fosse in time to tag Rose out, but Rose bowled Fosse over. Both players were injured, and Fosse dropped a perfect throw from Royals centerfielder Amos Otis, giving Rose credit for the game-winning run.

BASEBALL TRIVIA

• *Pete Rose is the all-time MLB leader in hits — 4,255.*

• *Fosse suffered a fractured and separated shoulder and never returned to his All-Star form.*

• *This was the first MLB All-Star Game ever played at night. Every All Star game since has been played at night.*

AL   ALL-STAR GAME   NL

INNINGS

8   10   6

TEN HOMERUNS-ALL-STAR GAME

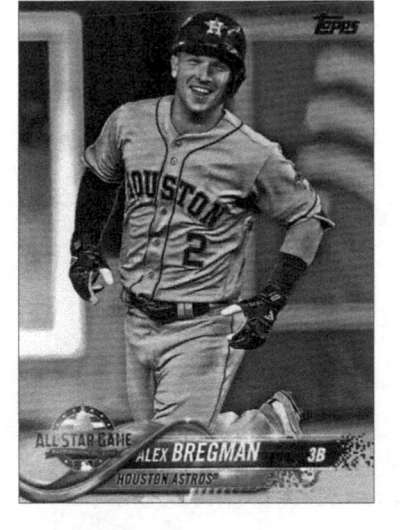

ALEX BREGMAN   3B
HOUSTON ASTROS

All but one of the runs in this game were a result of a homer. In the top of the 10th the AL scored 3 runs, two on home runs, off consecutive pitches: one by George Springer and the other by teammate Alex Bregman, which won the game. Bregman was named All Star game MVP.

BASEBALL TRIVIA

• *Entering the game, the AL and NL were tied with 43-43-2 records and had 361 runs scored in All Star history.*

• *This game had a record 10 home runs. The previous record was six. Each league had 5 round-trippers: AL: Aaron Judge, Mike Trout, Jean Segura, Alex Bregman, George Springer, and for the NL: Willson Contreras, Trevor Story, Christian Yelich, Scooter Gannett, Joey Votto. Justin Verland claimed the crazy number of home runs in this game proved the baseball was juiced.*

• *Justin Verlander is a six-time All-Star, three-time Cy Young winner, and has had three no-hitters.*

• *All but one run was scored by way of a home run, and each side scored the same number of run at 361.*

• *This was the second consecutive game the AL won in the 10th inning.*

PERFECT GAME NOT ENOUGH

In the 3rd inning, a base-run-ning blunder negated three consec-utive singles. In the 9th, Pittsburgh finally advanced a runner as far as third base, and in the 10th, pinch hitter Dick Stuart came within a few feet of ending Braves Lou Burdette's shutout bid with a two-run homer.

HARVEY HADDIX
PITTSBURGH PIRATES   PITCHER

Pirates lefty Harvey Haddix retired 36 batters in a row, but a fielding error by Don Hoak ended the per-fect game in the bottom of the 13th, with the leadoff batter for Milwaukee, Félix Mantilla, reaching first base. In the bottom of the 13th with 2 runners on base, Joe Adcock cleared the bases with a home run, but passed Hank Aaron, who had been walked before him, on the base paths on his way to second base, resulting in the home run being changed to a double. Braves Lou Burdette pitched 13 scoreless innings for the win.

BASEBALL TRIVIA

• *Pirates lefty Harvey Haddix retired 36 batters in a row in 12 innings, a Major League record, but the Pirates still lost this game.*

• *Lou Burdette had 203 career wins and was known for throwing a "spitball."*

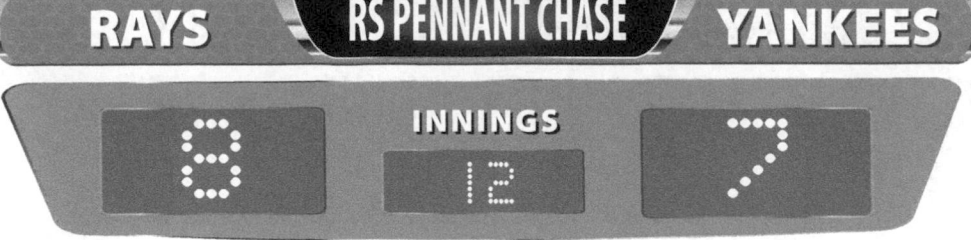
WILD CARD DESTINY

The Rays trailed 5–0 after just two innings. Going into the 8th inning, the Rays loaded the bases with no outs. Pinch hitter Sam Fuld then drew a bases-loaded walk to drive in the Rays' first run of the game. Sean Rodriguez was then hit by a pitch to score the second run.

With the score at 7–3, Evan Longoria came to the plate and hit the first pitch over the left field wall for a three-run home run that cut the deficit to 7–6. Then in the bottom of the 9th pinch hitter Dan Johnson hit a home run on a 2–2 count to tie the game at 7.

The Rays capped their comeback in the bottom of the 12th when Evan Longoria stepped to the plate and hit a walk-off home run down the left field line which barely cleared the lowest wall in the park, giving the Rays an 8–7 victory, giving them the AL Wild Card entry.

BASEBALL TRIVIA

• *Tropicana Field had 162 Landing, a designation in the left field corner where Longoria's playoff-clinching home run landed.*

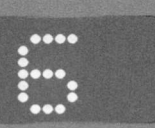

CUBS

NLDS-GAME 4

GIANTS

6   INNINGS   **5**

9

GIANTS FINALLY LOSE ELIMINATION GAME

The Giants, looking to win their 11th consecutive postseason elimination game, were comfortably ahead 5–2 heading to the top of the 9th. Cubs Manager Joe Madden and Giants Manager Bruce Bochy switched pitchers and pinch-hitters after the Cubs scored once and had runners on second and third.

Rookie catcher Willson Contreras single to center and scored 2 runs for the tie. Later in the inning, a single by 2nd baseman Javier Baez put the Cubs ahead 6–5.

The Cubs' high-priced closer, Aroldis Chapman, struck out the side in the bottom of the 9th.

GYPSY QUEEN

BAEZ, J., CUBS

BASEBALL TRIVIA

• *Baez is a 2-time All-Star (2018, 2019), World Series champion (2016), NLCS MVP (2016), won the Silver Slugger Award in 2018, and was NL RBI leader (2018).*

• *On September 24, 2010, against the San Diego Padres, Chapman was clocked at 105.1 mph (169.1 km/h), according to PITCHf/x, the fastest pitch ever recorded in Major League Baseball.*

STRIKING OUT'S A GOOD THING

"MICKEY" OWEN

In the "Subway Series" the Dodgers were 1 strike away from victory at home. Hugh "Fireman" Casey was on the mound, with no runners on base and Yankees right-fielder Tommy "Old-Reliable" Heinrich at bat with a full count.

Heinrich appeared to strike out, but Dodgers catcher Mickey Owens was charged with a passed ball error, allowing Heinrich to reach first base.

When the dust settled, the Yankees had scored 4 runs for the victory: Joe DiMaggio, with a single; Charlie "King Kong" Keller a double; Bill Dickey, a walk; and a Joe Gordon, a double.

Ironically, Owens was an All-Star catcher who in 1941 broke the record for most errorless fielding plays. As NYT sportswriter Red Smith remarked, "Only in the ancestral home of the Dodgers could a man win a game by striking out."

	INNINGS	
1	16	0

"THE SAY HAY KID"

Juan Marichal took the Candlestick Park mound. Four hours and 15 innings later, he was still toiling there, and so was Warren Spahn. The two were in a scoreless pitching duel.

In the 16th, Marichal allowed a two-out single and then registered his 48th out of the night on Larker's comebacker to the mound. It was Marichal's 227th pitch.

When the Giants hit, Spahn retired Harvey Kuenn on a fly out. That brought up future Hall of Famer Willie Mays, who was hitless so far in this game.

WILLIE
MAYS
S. F. GIANTS   OF

"The Say Hay Kid" Mays drove Spahn's first pitch in left, and the ball cleared the fence. With that, a masterfully-pitched game ended.

BASEBALL TRIVIA

• *Mays played 23 seasons, had 660 homeruns, a .302 career batting average, and 3,283 hits over 22 seasons.*

• *Juan Marichal threw 227 pitches in the game and had 243 career wins.*

• *The 42-year-old lefty, Warren Spahn, threw 201 pitches and had 365 career wins.*

IT WAS A NIGHTMARE

37. "WHITEY" WITT
Outfielder
N. Y. Yankees, A. L.

The defending AL champion Yankees and the hapless St. Louis Browns had been battling all season for the pennant, and it came down to the rubber game of a three-game series at Sportsman's Park in front of 30,000 fans, the biggest home crowd of the season and centerfield fans showed up wearing white shirts.

For seven innings Dixie Davis held the Yankees to just two hits, both of them infield hits by Whitey Witt. The Browns led 2–0.

In the 8th, Davis retired Witt for the first time that day. The Yankees scored a run on a "Jumpin'" Joe Dugan double and a Wally Pipp single.

In the 9th, the Yankees got all the breaks. Whitey Witt hit a pay-back single with bases loaded, scoring 2 runs for the victory. Commenting on this game's finish, *St. Louis Democrat* reporter John Sheridan said: "It was one of the most nerve-racking finishes ever flaunted before a St. Louis public. That one inning will remain indelible in the memory of the fans who witnessed it — to the grave. It was a nightmare."

"NAILS" GOES YARD

The Astros went ahead early 4–0, but 6'6" Mets left-handed hitting outfielder Darryl "The Straw Man" Strawberry hit a 3-run home run in the bottom half of the 6th. This highlighted a 4-run inning and tied the game.

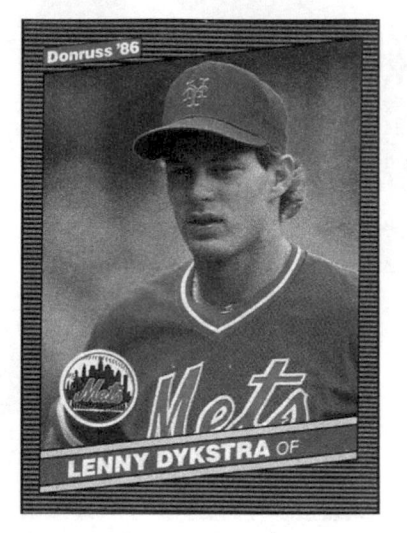

Donruss '86

LENNY DYKSTRA OF

The Astros struck back against reliever Rick Aguilera in the top of the 7th when a throwing error by Ray Knight led to an unearned run that came home when Denny Walling's fielder's choice scored Doran for a 5–4 lead.

In the bottom of the 9th, Closer Dave Smith allowed a lead-off bunt single to Wally Backman, who clearly ran out of the first-base line to avoid the tag, but was called safe.

Lenny "Nails" Dykstra then hit a two-run, walk-off homer, giving New York a 6–5 victory and 2–1 series lead.

BASEBALL TRIVIA

• *Years later, Dykstra, beset by financial difficulties, would spend 6-1/2 months in federal prison.*

• *Knight's gaffe was the only error committed by the Mets in the series.*

BRANDON BELT BELTS ONE

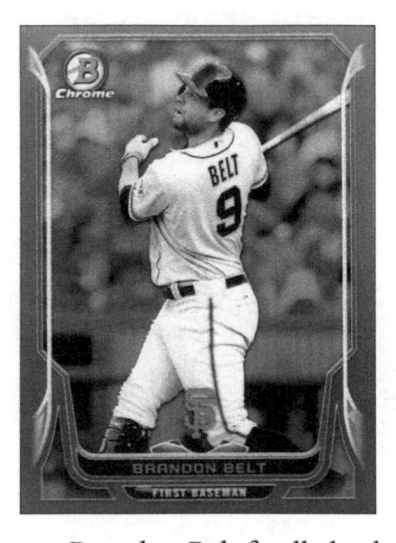

The game featured a pitching duel between Giants Tim Hudson, who struck out eight Nationals and conceded one run in 7-1/3 innings, and Nationals Ryan Zimmerman, who retired 20 Giants in a row.

The Giants rallied in the 9th when Buster Posey singled on the first pitch from closer Drew Storen, and Pablo Sandoval drove in Panik with a double. Posey was thrown out at home plate, and manager Bruce Bochy called for a video review but it was unsuccessful and it ended the inning.

Brandon Belt finally broke the tie, launching a home run off of Tanner Roark into the second deck in right field to lead off the 18th inning.

BASEBALL TRIVIA

• *This game was both the longest game in post season history, both by duration (6 hours 23 minutes) and innings played (18).*

SECOND GUESS DESERVED

Mariano Duncan's double and Madlock's single put the Dodgers ahead, 1–0. An inning later, a walk to Greg Brock and singles by Hershiser and Duncan scored Brock to give the Dodgers a 2–0 lead.

In the 9th, Tom Niedenfuer struck out César Cedeño, but McGee singled and stole second. With Ozzie Smith's prior success against Niedenfuer — a homer and triple in his last two at-bats — the Dodgers walked him and induced a ground out from Tommy Herr.

JACK CLARK
FIRST BASE

FLEER

With runners at second and third and two out, Jack Clark was next at bat. Manager Tommy Lasorda faced a dilemma, did he want to walk Clark or pitch him? Niedenfuer had struck out Clark in the 7th, and the next two hitters in the Cardinal line-up, Van Slyke and Pendleton, weren't a threat. Lasorda opted to pitch, and Clark proceeded to drill Niedenfuer's first fastball 450 feet into the left field stands for a pennant-winning home run.

16 RUN DEFICIT NO BIG DEAL

This Class A Midwest League early season game featured grand slams by both catchers, 19 unanswered runs by the winning team and a perfect save by a position player making his first appearance on a mound. All of this combined to make this one of the most remarkable games in minor league history.

The Burlington Bees, an Angels affiliate, scored nine times in the 5th inning, and delighted the crowd with a 17-1 lead punctuated by a grand slam off the bat of catcher Cambric Moye.

Everything went downhill from there for the Bees. The Clinton Lumberkings, a Mariners farm team, rallied for six runs in the sixth, but still trailed by 10 runs. The score was then 17–12 after a five-run 8th inning.

Alan Busenitz was brought in to replace Ben Carlson, who had allowed four straight singles. Busenitz faced catcher Marcus Littlewood, and was promptly greeted with a game-tying grand slam. After blowing a 16-run lead, the game was tied at 17.

Both teams were scoreless in the next two innings. In the 12th, Justin Seager grounded out to score the go-ahead run, then second baseman Lonnie Kauppila singled home two more runs to make it 20-17 Clinton.

"THE BIG TILDE"

Mark Kotsay walked with one out in the first off Jeremy Bonderman, then scored on Milton Bradley's double. One out later, Bradley scored on Eric Chavez's double to put Oakland up 2-0. Jay Payton homered in the 4th to make it 3–0.

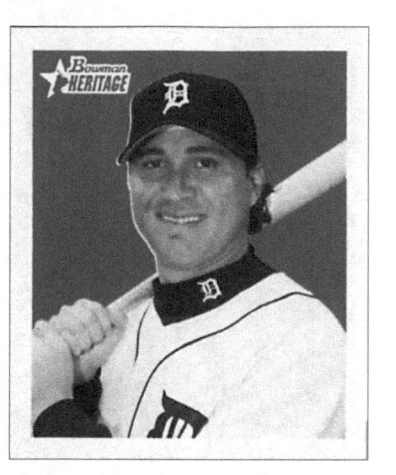

Magglio Ordóñez homered in the 6th to tie the game at three. In the bottom of the 9th, Huston Street got two outs, then allowed back-to-back singles to Polanco and Monroe before Ordóñez launched a three-run walk-off home run to win the game and advance the Tigers to the 2006 World Series.

BASEBALL TRIVIA

• Ordóñez's blast was the first pennant-winning home run since Aaron Boone's in Game 7 of the 2003 ALCS and came on the 30th Anniversary of Chris Chambliss' pennant-winning walk-off in Game 5 of the 1976 ALCS.

• Ordóñez finished his career with a lifetime batting average of .309. After retiring, he returned home to Venezuela where he became the mayor of a local municipality in 2013.

RANKING
86
OCTOBER 10, 2016
GIANTS   NLDS-GAME 3   CUBS
INNINGS
6   13   5

GIANTS AVOID SWEEP

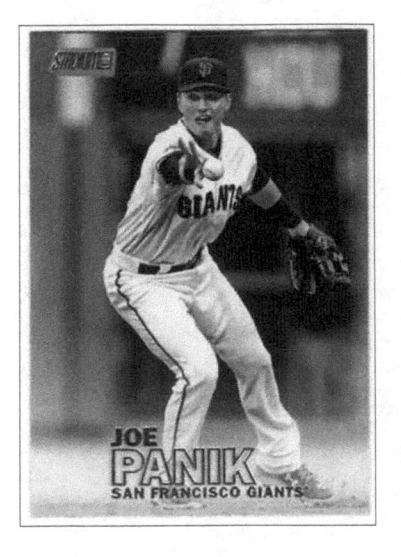

The Giants, hoping to avoid a sweep while extending their streak to 10–0 in elimination games, won their only game of the series after trailing 3–0 on a 3-run homer off the bat of Cubs' starting pitcher Jake Arrieta in the top of the second.

The Giants chipped away with single runs in the 3rd and 5th and out came the Cubs Aroldis Chapman in the 8th inning, seeking a six-out save surrendering a two-out triple, giving the Giants a 4–3 lead. Brandon Crawford drove in another, and San Francisco looked poised to win the game. But Kris Bryant hit a two-run shot to left in the top of the 9th off closer Sergio Romo to bring the game back even at 5–5.

In the 13th, the Giants Joe Panik hit a walk-off double to right field, scoring Brandon Crawford, to give the Giants a walk-off 6–5 win over the Cubs

ASTRODOME OPENS

The Houston Astrodome's official opening featured an exhibition game between the Astros and Yankees. Yankees first run, which turned out to be their only score, was fittingly a solo home run by Mickey Mantle in the top of the 6th.

In the bottom of the 12th, the Astros broke the 1-1 tie off Pete Mikkelsen. Jimmy Wynn started with an infield single, stole second, and with 2 outs was driven in by 37-year-old second baseman and Yankees nemesis Nellie Fox on a bloop single to center.

BASEBALL TRIVIA

• *The Astrodome, the world's first multipurpose dome was nicknamed the "Eighth Wonder of the World."*

• *The Astrodome was a pitcher's delight; the ball didn't carry and the hitters had poor visibility.*

RANKING
88
JULY 12, 1994
ALL-STAR GAME
NL   AL
INNINGS
8   10   7

TONY GWYNN WITH HIS LEGS

The NL ended a 6-game losing streak that ended with this 10-inning win.

In the 3rd inning, Tony "Mr. Padre" Gwynn's double to the right field corner scored two, giving the NL a 4–1 lead through 5 innings.

A home run from Toronto's Fred McGriff tied the game in the 9th sending the game in to extra innings.

In the 10th, the NL quickly went to work on AL reliever Jason Bere of the White Sox. Gwynn chopped a single through the box with no one out. The Expos' Moisés Alou then slammed a double that short-hopped the left center field wall. Gwynn was waved home from first base and slid in just under Pudge Rodriguez's tag to end the game.

BASEBALL TRIVIA

• *Hall of Famer Tony Gwynn spent his entire 19-year career with the Padres, and had a .338 career batting average, 3,141 hits, was league batting champion eight times, and was a 15-time All-Star. In the shortened 1994 season Gwynn batted .394 coming clost to .400, which as last hit in 1941.*

"BLEEPIN'" BUCKY DENT

The Yankees and Red Sox finished the season at identical 99–63 records, after the Yankees had trailed by 14 games in mid-July when Yankees owner George "The Boss" Steinbrenner replaced his controversial Manager Billy Martin with Bob Lemon.

The Red Sox led 2–0 behind starter Mike Torres when Yankees light hitting shortstop Bucky Dent, who had 5 home runs all season, came to bat in the top of the 7th with Chris Chambliss and Roy White on base. Bucky hit a fly ball into the friendly left field screen at Fenway Park for a 3-run home run.

BUCKY DENT

The Yankees would add a single run in the 8th with the Sox adding 2 runs in the bottom of the frame. The Sox came to bat in the 9th, needing a run for the tie. With Rick Burleson on first, Jerry Remy's single to right should have sent Burleson to third, except Yankees right fielder "Sweet" Lou Piniella, pretending to catch the ball by pounding his glove, decoyed Burleson, who held at second. When AL MVP and HOF outfielder Jim Rice followed with a deep fly to the outfield, Burleson could only move up to third base instead of scoring the tying run.

"THE STEVE BARTMAN INCIDENT

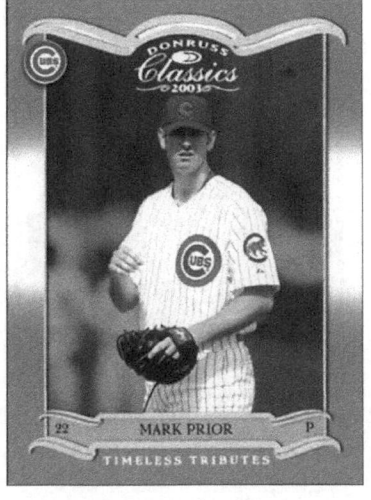

With thousands of fans on the street outside sold-out Wrigley Field, poised to celebrate, the Cubs held a 3–0 lead going into the top of the 8th. After Mike Mordecai hit a high pop fly to left field, the team was a mere five outs away from their first World Series since 1945. Mark Prior had retired the last eight hitters and had allowed only three hits up to that point. Center fielder Juan Pierre then hit a double off Prior.

In the 8th, all hell broke loose after Luis Castillo hit a high foul ball toward the left field wall. Cubs left fielder Moisés Alou headed toward the stands to catch it. As Alou reached for it, Cubs fan Steve Bartman did the same. The umpire ruled the ball was in the stands rather than calling fan interference. When Castillo came to bat for the second time in the 8th, to make the last out, the Marlins had scored 8 runs, sending the NCS to a deciding game seven.

THE 'MAJOR' GETS LUCKY

Yankees Ralph Terry, pitching in place of Jim Bouton because of a rain postponement, took a 4-hit shutout in to the bottom of the 9th leading 1-0. He would have to face the Giants' three Hall of Famers: Willie Mays, Willie McCovey, and Orlando Cepeda.

The first batter, Matty Alou, laid down a bunt single, and then after the next two batters struck out, Mays followed with a double to right. Right fielder Roger Maris played the carom off the wall perfectly, forcing Alou to hold at third.

With runners on 2nd and 3rd and 2 outs, Yankees Manager Ralph "The Major" Houk elected to pitch to the lefty "Stretch" McCovey. McCovey hit a frozen rope to Yankees second sacker Bobby Richardson, who was positioned perfectly and never moved a muscle.

BASEBALL TRIVIA

• *Ralph Houk, the successor of Casey Stengel, was a Major in WWII and a 3rd string catcher.*

• *Ralph Terry, who later became a professional golfer, was named the World Series MVP.*

28-OUT PERFECT GAME

So-so pitcher Armando Galarraga nearly became the 21st pitcher in Major League history to throw a perfect game.

With this career outing, Galarraga was on his way to the Hall of Fame. He was denied a perfect game by first base Umpire Jim Joyce, who ruled Jason Donald safe after a routine ground ball. (Replays showed he was out.)

Joyce was tearful and apologetic to Galarraga after the game, upon realizing he had made the incorrect call. Galarraga was forgiving and understanding of the mistake, and told reporters after the game, "Nobody's perfect."

Though Galarraga was missed the perfect game by just one out, he is credited with a one-hit shutout, having thrown just 88 pitches and faced 28 batters.

NO-HITTER NEEDED

Christy "The Gentlemen's Hurler" Mathewson pitched his second career no-hitter. Christy bested the Cubs Mordecai "Three Finger" Brown 1–0 on a hit by shortstop "Bad Bill" Dahlen in the top of the 9th.

BASEBALL TRIVIA

MATHEWSON, N. Y. NAT'L

• *Each of the five games was a shutout. Three of those, over a six-day span, were pitched and won by Christy Mathewson.*

• *Mathewson pitched his entire 17-year career for the New York Giants*

• *He ranks in the all-time top 10 in several key pitching categories, including wins, shutouts, and ERAs.*

• *In 1936, Mathewson was elected into the Baseball Hall of Fame as one of its first five members.*

• *Brown lost fingers in his right hand, his throwing hand, in a farm's food chopper accident, but learned how to throw a 'knuckle' curve which became his out pitch.*

• *Mathewson and Brown had one of the greatest pitching rivalries in history. Both combined for 612 career wins and made it to the Hall of Fame.*

TWINS HARD LUCK LOSS

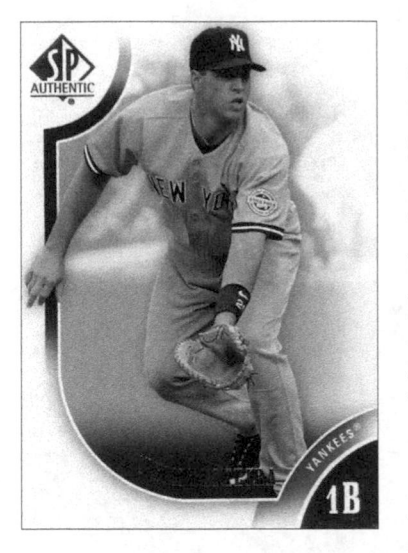

Alex "A-Rod" Rodriguez, one of the all-time greats, hit a tying single in the bottom of the 6th and a 2-run home run in the 9th, to send the game in to extra innings.

Yankees All-Star first baseman Mark Teixeira hit a walk-off home run in the bottom of the 11th. The Twins, who had a history of playing the Yankees tough in the postseason but always losing, appeared to have gone ahead in the top of the 11th.

Umpire Phil Cuzzi blew the call on catcher Joe Mauer's double attempt. Yankees reliever Dave Robertson was then able to escape from a bases loaded jam. The Twins out-hit the Yankees 12-7, but left 17 runners on base.

BASEBALL TRIVIA

• *A-Rod's career included a batting average of .295, 3,115 hits, 696 home runs, and 2,086 RBIs. His accomplishments include: 14-time All Star, 2009 World Series champion, 3-time AL MVP, 2-time Gold Glove Award, 10-time Silver Slugger Award, 4-time AL Hank Aaron Award, 1996 MLB batting champion, 5-time AL home run leader, and 2-time MLB RBI leader. Because of steroids, his career will always be followed by an asterisk.*

THE MIRACLE BRAVES

The A's Frank "Homerun" Baker singled in the top of the 10th and scored 2 runs, giving the A's a 4–2 lead.

In the bottom of the 10th Hank Gowdy's lead-off home run was followed by Joe Connolly's sacrifice fly, tying the contest. Game 2 winner Bill James came on in relief for the win. The win came after Gowdy doubled and pinch-runner Les Mann scored when starter "Bullet" Joe Bush misplayed a bunt by Herbie Moran tossing wildly pass 3rd base.

The Braves, in last place and without a home field, swept the heavily favored A's in 4 games. The A's, built by Connie

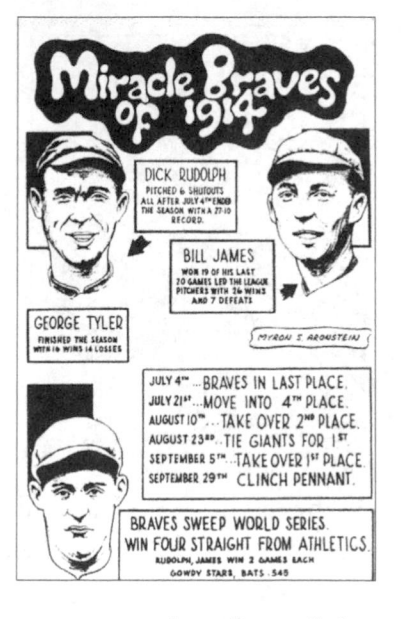

Mack, won 6 pennants from 1902–1914. Rumors strongly indicated this Series was fixed.

BASEBALL TRIVIA

• *After the Series, due to financial issues, Mack had to disband his ball club.*

• *Baker, who was called the "original home run king of the majors" led the American League in home runs for four consecutive years, from 1911 through 1914.*

PHILLIES — LAST GAME OF SEASON — DODGERS

	INNINGS	
4	10	1

"PITCHOUT LUCKY"

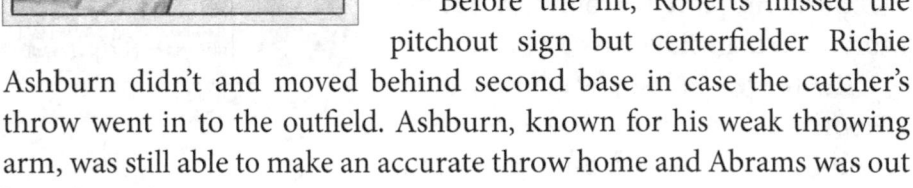

On the last day of the regular season, the "Whiz Kids" needed a win in Brooklyn against the mighty Dodgers if they were to avoid a three-game playoff against the same Dodgers.

In the bottom of the 9th, the speedy Cal Abrams was on second when Duke "The Duke of Flatbush" Snider hit a single to centerfield off Robin Roberts the Phillies All-Star starter.

Before the hit, Roberts missed the pitchout sign but centerfielder Richie Ashburn didn't and moved behind second base in case the catcher's throw went in to the outfield. Ashburn, known for his weak throwing arm, was still able to make an accurate throw home and Abrams was out by 15'.

In the top of the 10th, Dick Sisler hit a 3-run homerun for the win and the pennant.

BASEBALL TRIVIA

• *Dick Sisler, heor of the game, was the son of Hall of Famer George Sisler, who at the time was chief scout for the Brooklyn Dodgers.*

WILDEST GAME EVER

The wind blowing out 18 mph set the stage for this high scoring affair at Wrigley. Phillies HOF 3rd sacker Mike Schmidt blasted 2 home runs in the game, second in the top of the 10th, that decided the outcome.

MIKE SCHMIDT 3B
PHILLIES

The Phillies scored seven runs in the first inning on the strength of three home runs: a two-run shot from Mike Schmidt, a two-run shot from Bob Boone and a solo homer from pitcher Randy Lerch. The Cubs answered with six runs in the bottom half, which included 6'6" Dave "King Kong" Kingman's first of three homers on the day.

Heading to the bottom of the fifth, the Phillies led 21-9. But in the 10th, future Hall of Famer Schmidt went deep off future Hall of Famer Bruce Sutter to give the Phillies a 23-22 lead and eventual win.

BASEBALL TRIVIA

• *Stats for this game: 50 combined hits, 45 runs, 11 home runs, 127 batters and 11 pitchers.*

• *Dave Kingman and .442 career homeruns and the 4th most strikeouts in history.*

WHITE SOX — WORLD SERIES-GAME 6 — REDS

INNINGS

5   10   4

BLACK SOX SCANDAL

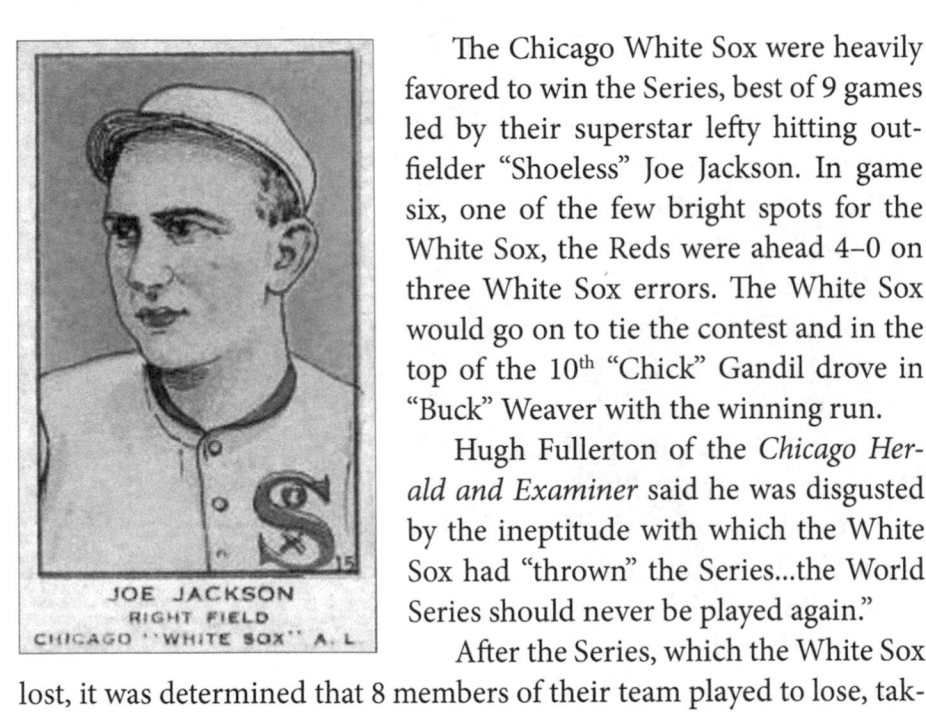

JOE JACKSON
RIGHT FIELD
CHICAGO "WHITE SOX" A. L.

The Chicago White Sox were heavily favored to win the Series, best of 9 games led by their superstar lefty hitting out-fielder "Shoeless" Joe Jackson. In game six, one of the few bright spots for the White Sox, the Reds were ahead 4–0 on three White Sox errors. The White Sox would go on to tie the contest and in the top of the 10th "Chick" Gandil drove in "Buck" Weaver with the winning run.

Hugh Fullerton of the *Chicago Herald and Examiner* said he was disgusted by the ineptitude with which the White Sox had "thrown" the Series...the World Series should never be played again."

After the Series, which the White Sox lost, it was determined that 8 members of their team played to lose, taking orders from gambler Arnold Rothstein. Those 8players received lifetime bans for game fixing.

BASEBALL TRIVIA

• *Joe Jacksn's lifetime batting average was .356.*

LONGHORNS · COLLEGE WORLD SERIES · EAGLES

	INNINGS	
3	25	2

GRASS GROWS EVER SO SLOWLY

The longest game in the history of college baseball concluded at 2:05 Sunday morning. Texas won on a 1 out single by Travis Tucker, following a Connor Rowe walk, a sacrifice, and a wild pitch won the game.

The star of the game was Texas reliever Austin Woods, who pitched 13 innings, 12-1/3 of no-hit ball. In total, Woods threw 169 pitches, 120 of which were called strikes.

Texas Coach Augie Garrido, the winningest coach in the history of college

EXTRA EDITION

AUSTIN WOOD
DETROIT · PITCHER

baseball (1817-825-81), called Wood's performance "the greatest he had ever seen."

VLAD'S CATCH THE DIFFERENCE

VLADIMIR GUERRERO
Outfielder • EXPOS™

The Phillies led 8–0, when in the bottom of the 5th, Vladimir Guerrero led off with a single. Wil Cordero singled to right, sending Guerrero to second. Todd Zeile, just signed as a free agent on August 20, singled to load the bases. Brian Schneider grounded out to first, scoring Guerrero. Endy Chavez grounded out to short, scoring Cordero. Ron Calloway, pinch-hitting for Knott, stroked a base hit to right, scoring Zeile. Brad Wilkerson lined out to end the inning but not before the Expos got on the board and closed the gap to 8-3.

After the Expos scored 7-runs in the last of the 7th to lead 11-10, the big play of the game turned out to be a defensive gem in the 8th inning. HOF right fielder Guerrero made a spectacular catch by climbing the wall, preventing at least 2 runs from scoring. The Expos scored three more in the bottom of the 8th, highlighted by Cordero's two-run double, to make the score 14–10.

BASEBALL TRIVIA

• *"Vlad" Guerrero is best known for being baseball's premier "bad ball hitter."*